ADVANCE

C000022596

"Giles's new collection of brand tales is an enjoyable and accessible read that demonstrates how innovation can come from anywhere. A great insight into how brands we're all familiar with have found inspiration."
Richard Underhill, European Consumer Research Manager, Sony Computer Entertainment

"Giles has once again unearthed a range of engaging, funny and educational stories that anyone interested in the world of brands will enjoy. On top of this, many of the themes dominating marketing discourse today can be traced through this book – gender balance, racial inequality and political volatility to name but a few – with direct implications for the work many of us are doing today."
Nick Holden, Consumer Insight Controller, Premier Foods

Published by
LID Publishing Limited
The Record Hall, Studio 204,
16-16a Baldwins Gardens,
London EC1N 7RJ, UK

524 Broadway, 11th Floor, Suite 08-120,
New York, NY 10012, US

info@lidpublishing.com
www.lidpublishing.com

A member of:

www.businesspublishersroundtable.com

© Giles Lury, 2019
© LID Publishing Limited, 2019

Printed in Great Britain by TJ International
ISBN: 978-1-912555-05-5

Illustration: Guy Chalkley
Cover and Page design: Caroline Li & Matthew Renaudin

INSPIRING INNOVATION

75 MARKETING TALES
TO HELP YOU FIND THE NEXT BIG THING

GILES LURY

LONDON   NEW YORK   SHANGHAI
MADRID   BARCELONA   BOGOTA
MEXICO CITY   MONTERREY   BUENOS AIRES

DEDICATION

For the crazy ones, the misfits,
the rebels and troublemakers everywhere.

TABLE OF CONTENTS

INTRODUCTION

Where do ideas come from?

It is commonly thought that 90% of new products and services fail, although a number of recent studies suggest that the figure is a little lower, at around 70%.* However, it's still depressingly high.

This book celebrates the people and ideas behind the 30%, the minority.

They are what Apple called 'the crazy ones' in the tech company's famous 1997 *Think Different* ad.

> Here's to the crazy ones.
> The misfits.
> The rebels.
> The troublemakers.
> The round pegs in the square holes.
> The ones who see things differently.
> They're not fond of rules, and they have
> no respect for the status quo.
> You can quote them, disagree with them,
> glorify or vilify them.
> But the only thing you can't do is ignore them.
> Because they change things.
> They push the human race forward.
> And while some may see them as
> the crazy ones, we see genius.
> Because the people who are crazy enough to think
> they can change the world are the ones who do.

This book is a collection of the stories behind some of the world's most famous brands, and their products and services. It introduces you to the crazies and not-so-crazy ones who decided to do something different, something new, who wanted to change things for the better.

In particular, the stories identify the many, varied, weird and wonderful sources of their original ideas, and as such can serve as a source of inspiration as you look for your company's (or your own personal) next big idea.

In marketing, innovation has become professionalized – it has structured and it has industrialized. There are stage gates and funnels, and many processes and tools packaged differently … but they're basically very similar.

Increasingly, the marketing mantra is that all innovation must start with the consumer. The consumer is king.

So, in practice you'll find many companies are:
    Asking their (same) consumers
    the same things,
    in similar ways,
    and not surprisingly, getting to the same ideas,
    at about the same time!

They say variety is the spice of life, but I believe it's the spice of innovation too. So, I feel that it's important to look at different starting points.

You can take either a brand-led approach or a technology-led approach to developing innovative ideas.

An example from my own experience is when McVitie's, the British biscuit brand, came to The Value Engineers and told us about their 'improved barrier technology'. Resisting the urge to say, "Good for you,"

I asked, "What does that actually mean?"

They explained that it was the ability to have more runny liquid layers in a product while avoiding the problem of a soggy bottom.

"Does this mean that you could add extra layers like toffee?" we asked.

"Of course," they replied.

From there it is perhaps not surprising that one of the first ideas in the ensuing workshop took the much loved McVitie's Digestives and mixed it with a millionaire's shortbread ... and the Caramel Digestive was born.

Insight from existing and parallel categories, and the application of science, were the real source of inspiration here.

The LEGO watch didn't start with the consumer. Children weren't crying out for another type of watch. It started with the brand. Creative, constructive and gently educational translates beautifully into the popular 'construct and re-construct' LEGO watches.

You don't have to start with the consumer but you do need ideas, which brings me back to the stories in this book.

Inspiring myself?

Before starting on the stories, experience from my previous books tells me that at some point I will be asked, "So where does the inspiration for this particular book come from?"

In this case it comes from two different yet interrelated sources. The first was my addiction to telling brand stories; the second was how I've found myself telling one of those stories time and time again.

I love stories of all shapes and sizes. I'm a sucker for sci-fantasy, thrillers and love both Disney and Pixar.

I'm not sure I'll ever write a novel, but over the years my love of stories has been combined with my day job as a brand consultant and I've collected, told and re-told countless marketing tales.

I've told all sorts of brand-related stories, but the one I have found myself coming back to begins on an aeroplane.

It was the late 1960s and a young chemist was flying to a meeting. Sitting next to him was a woman who, as they came in to land, began putting on her make-up. The young man found himself fascinated by what she was doing – the way she applied her lipstick, twisting the tube to push the lipstick up so that she could easily apply it to her lips.

No fuss, no messy colour on her hands, and a nice, smooth, even finish.

The proverbial light bulb went off. He was a chemist for Henkel, the German chemical and consumer goods company, and he realized that he may have found the answer to a problem – the application of glue, traditionally a messy and difficult job.

Pritt Stick, the world's first glue stick, was launched in 1969 and is still going strong today.

This little tale is typical of the stories I tell. It's short and delivers an implicit lesson – a marketing 'moral'.

In this case, the moral is how inspiration can strike anytime, anywhere, so to be a good innovator you should remain constantly curious.

Thinking about why I've told this particular story so often, it struck me that one of the reasons is that it is about innovation. Finding new ideas and bringing them to market is one of the most important roles a marketer has to play, and it's also one of the most difficult. Any thoughts, ideas and inspiration are therefore welcome.

So I decided that for this collection of stories I would focus on innovation, tell some wonderful anecdotes, demonstrate that there are lots of different ways of getting inspired and discuss the tools needed to turn your idea into a reality.

For example, when the comedian Jerry Seinfeld was interviewed by *Harvard Business Review* about his insights into innovation, he talked about the development of his award-winning, ground-breaking 'Seinfeld' series. He explained, "It is very important to know what you don't like," and said he believed that "a big part of innovation starts with someone saying, 'You know what I'm sick of'?"

Here was a first-rate innovator talking about innovation without mentioning the consumer or, in his case, 'the viewer'. Here was someone talking about different ways in which innovation happens.

Consequently, as a believer that there is rarely one right answer in marketing, it further confirmed my desire to share a few stories to illustrate the point.

In this book I've included stories about how sometimes you find what you're *not* looking for (Viagra), how innovators find inspiration in the strangest of places (like in jail) and how you can innovate by helping the one you love (Maybelline).

Innovation comes in many different forms, from incremental to breakthrough. Likewise, inspiration can come from a variety of sources, and while you must always address a customer need in the end, you don't need to start with customer insight.

As with my previous book of stories I have included a moral at the end of each tale, although this time I've called them 'Sparkpoints' as that's what they are supposed to do – spark your imagination. They are my take on a lesson or technique you could adopt, but feel free to find your own.

August 2018

* Stanton, John. "New Product Success Rate Higher Than Most Believe", *Food Processing* (Mar 27 2014) https://www.foodprocessing.com/articles/2014/new-product-success-rate-higher-than-most-believe/.

THE STORIES

1. THE SAMPLES THEY WOULDN'T GIVE BACK

The fastest selling drug of all time doesn't do what it was originally intended to do.

It started life in 1989 as a medication called sildenafil citrate and was classified as UK-92480. It had been created by British scientists, Peter Dunn and Albert Wood, working for Pfizer. They believed it would be useful in treating high blood pressure and angina, chest pain caused by the constriction of vessels that supply the heart with blood.

Somewhat disappointingly for them, and for Pfizer, the initial trial results suggested that it didn't help relax these blood vessels.

However, things were looking up on another front as Dr Brian Klee, a senior medical director at Pfizer, later told the French news agency, AFP: "Originally, we were testing sildenafil ... as a cardiovascular drug and for its ability to lower blood pressure, but one thing that was found during those trials is that people didn't want to give the medication back because of the side effect of having erections that were harder, firmer and lasted longer."

With UK-92480's chances of treating angina slim, Pfizer decided to focus on erectile dysfunction, so another Pfizer scientist, Chris Wayman, was asked to investigate what was happening.

He created a model 'man' in the lab.

He took a set of test tubes filled with an inert solution and placed a piece of penile tissue taken from an impotent man in each one. Each piece of tissue was then connected up to a device that, at the flick of a switch, would send a pulse of electricity through it.

Applying this current of electricity mimicked what happens when a man is aroused.

The first time Chris did this nothing happened to the vessels, but when he added the drug to the tissue bath the penile blood vessels suddenly relaxed – as they would for a man with normal erectile function – giving him an erection.

"What was amazing about this study was that we saw a restoration of the erectile response," he said. "Now we were on to something which could only be described as special."

In 1996 Pfizer, on the back of further encouraging test results, patented sildenafil citrate in the US.

On 27 March 1998, complete with a new name, the FDA approved the use of the drug Viagra to treat erectile dysfunction.

It's estimated that the drug has now been used by more than 35 million men around the world.

SPARKPOINT: *Sometimes you can start out looking for one thing but find another along the way – don't ignore happy accidents.*

2. DRAWN TO THE TABLE BY THE 'LUR' OF GREAT BUTTER

What is a lur?

A lur, or lur horn, is a type of cast bronze wind instrument that originated in the Late Bronze Age (1,000 BC). It consists of an s-shaped pipe made of several pieces of bronze that have been welded together, a soundboard at the upper end and a mouthpiece at the lower end.

Most of the lurs that have been found have come from Denmark, though some have also been found in Sweden, Norway and northern Germany. The curving shape of the tubes recalls ox horns, on which the ancient lurs are thought to have been modelled.

The name 'lur' is of more recent origin. It was first used by archaeologists at the beginning of the 19th century.

They took it from the Icelandic sagas, which say that "warriors were summoned to battle with the lur."

In recent times the lur has often been used as a motif and has become linked with Denmark and Danish quality. It has been used in political contexts and art. There is a famous statue of two lur-blowers in City Hall Square in Copenhagen.

Perhaps the most famous modern use of lurs is as a trademark.

In the late 19th century Danish butter had built up a reputation for being of the highest quality and of exceptional taste. Inevitably, many butters from other countries tried to pass themselves off as Danish.

Danish dairy farmers came together and decided something had to be done to protect their reputation and their trade. So, on 23 October 1901, 'Lurmark' was registered as the trademark for quality Danish butter.

In 1957 Lurmark Danish Butter became the Lurpak brand that we know and love today. It is still owned by the Danish Dairy Board cooperative which, in turn, is part of Arla Foods, and is sold in 75 countries worldwide.

The brand identity still features entwined lurs as a symbol of that Danish quality, to summon not Icelandic warriors to battle but food lovers to the table.

They will be drawn by the lur(e) of the great taste of the finest Danish butter.

> **SPARKPOINT:** *If you have a great idea make sure you do everything to 'own' it, and to protect your ownership of it.*

3. SELLING LIKE WILDFIRE

You've probably experienced it … perhaps on a weekly basis. You're dashing off to a meeting or preparing for that big presentation when the photocopier jams and the dreaded error sign appears.

How do you feel?

Well, you're not alone. According to an article in *The Wall Street Journal*,* printers are among the most in-demand objects in 'rage rooms', where people pay to smash things with sledgehammers and baseball bats.

Battle Sports in Toronto goes through 15 printers a week. In the UK, a new gaming centre in Birmingham lets you smash up a desktop printer for just £10.

Yet, the paper jam is one of the more recent first-world problems. Gutenberg invented his printing press around 1440 but the modern paper jam didn't arrive until around 1960.

Gutenberg's printing press was considerably slower than its modern-day counterparts but, because printing was done one sheet at a time, jamming was impossible. With the first presses, inked type was lowered onto individual sheets of paper and, even with later versions that used a rotary drum, the paper was hand-fed to avoid jamming.

In 1863, an inventor and newspaper editor named William Bullock created what became known as the Bullock Press. Beyond the innovation of the rotary drum, it was fed by a single, continuous roll of paper. Some of those rolls were up to several miles long. This dramatically increased the speed of the printing and made the machine a great success. Unfortunately, William wasn't to benefit from it for long. In 1867 one of his legs got caught in the press, which would have been bad enough, but the wound became gangrenous and he died.

The next major step forward came in 1938 with the application of xerography, which gives you a clue as to which brand was leading this development.

In xerography, static electricity quickly and precisely manipulates electrostatically sensitive powdered ink – what we know as toner. As the term 'photocopier' suggests, a xerographic machine is less like a traditional printer and more like a darkroom.

Chester Carlson was the physicist and co-founder of Xerox who invented their first xerography machines. To work these copiers, you placed your original under a glass pane, where light was reflected onto a statically charged photosensitive plate. The charged plate then drew toner from a tray and transferred the toned image to plain paper. Finally, the toner was 'melted' into the paper in what amounted to a miniature electric oven. Each copy took around three minutes to make.

By 1959 the company had managed to automate the process and introduced the Xerox 914, the world's first automatic office copier. It could deliver seven copies a minute.

They also realized that there was a potential snag, as the new model had a mildly concerning side effect – the paper jam. It was a problem that wasn't just frustrating but potentially dangerous, as jammed paper combined with the heating element sometimes set the paper on fire.

No easy solution was found, but that didn't stop the launch. Xerox merely shipped the first models complete with free fire extinguishers.

Despite this, the Xerox 914 was a huge success – between 1960 and 1979 it generated around $40 billion in sales … along with one or two fires.

SPARKPOINT: *Sometimes it's better to go with something that is 80% right than continue to strive for 100% perfect. You might never get there.*

* Olson, Bradley and Randazzo, Sara. "Do You Really, Truly Hate Your Office Printer? There's a Bat for That," *The Wall Street Journal* (Aug 24 2016), https://www.wsj.com/articles/think-your-office-printer-deserves-a-good-beating-theres-a-bat-for-that-1472048959.

4. BEHEADING – AN UNUSUAL SOURCE OF INSPIRATION

Even though I can't sing, someone was once kind enough to call me 'the minstrel of marketing' because wherever I go I spread little stories about brands and branding. While I like researching and writing my own version of these stories, sometimes you come across one that's just perfect as it is.

And so it was when I stumbled across the story of Penguin.

No, not the publisher – I've already told that story in a previous book. Nor was it the story of the chocolate biscuit, which might be one to research for another time.

This story deals with the origins of the Original Penguin clothing brand and resides on their website.

Now, if anyone had told me that the inspiration for a brand I sometimes wear was the beheading of a penguin named Pete, I'm not sure I would have believed them ... but read on.

"In 1955, an ambitious salesman named Abbot Pederson travelled to New York City on a sales trip for the Munsingwear brand," goes the origin story. "With time to kill before a flight home, he decided to pop into a local bar for a few whiskeys. Little did he know, his next steps would stumble into history."

Taking a wrong turn down a Manhattan street, he oddly enough found himself outside a taxidermist's shop. Deciding he needed a drinking buddy for the flight, he bought a stuffed penguin and named him Pete. At some point during the flight, and after another cocktail or three, he accidentally knocked Pete's head off.

A stewardess removed Abbot's necktie and wrapped it around the penguin's neck. She joked that such a dapper bird deserved to be immortalized, maybe even on a shirt. And with that idea, an icon was born.

Within a matter of years, the Munsingwear golf shirt embroidered with Pete's likeness had become synonymous with cool, pop-culture legends like Frank Sinatra, Dean Martin, Arnold Palmer and Clint Eastwood. Today, the Original Penguin clothing line embodies a mix of iconic American sportswear and modern-minded style, delivering a diverse range of products for a full lifestyle brand. 'Made for originals, by originals'.

SPARKPOINT: *People can be generous with their ideas; it doesn't cost anything to listen, and sometimes what they say can be of great value.*

Footnote: Subsequent research has shown me that there are other stories about the origins of this brand and its logo, but none are as much fun ... so I'm sticking with this one.

5. A STORY OF MEN AND LINGERIE AT CHRISTMAS

This is a story about when *it's that time of year again.*

The shelves are laden with tinsel and baubles, the old Christmas songs are playing on endless loops in lifts and plans are being made for the infamous office holiday party. And, you can expect every self-respecting tabloid to run a feature on why men are so bad at buying lingerie for their loved ones.

Seeing one of these articles reminded me of the beginnings of what is now one of the world's largest lingerie brands.

In 1969 Roy Raymond went to buy his wife Gaye a gift, an event that he recalled some years later in an interview with *Newsweek*: "When I tried to buy lingerie for my wife, I was faced with racks of terry-cloth robes and ugly floral-print nylon nightgowns, and I always had the feeling the department store saleswomen thought I was an unwelcome intruder."

It was an event that clearly scarred him. He decided something had to change and for the next eight years he studied the lingerie market, developing his ideas. Finally settling on a concept, he borrowed $40,000 from his parents and $40,000 from a bank to establish Victoria's Secret.

Roy's aim was to market women's lingerie to men, and he wanted to create a store in which men could feel comfortable buying these more intimate items. He wanted the stores to be places where men could browse at their leisure without having to manically flash their wedding bands or be constantly frowned upon.

Though American, Roy picked a name with a British twist. 'Victoria' was a reference to Queen Victoria and was chosen to bring with it associations of the style, elegance and class of the Victorian era. The 'Secret' was of course hidden underneath the clothes and probably in those olden days still seen as something mildly shocking.

The store design was an homage to the boudoir with hints of seduction, featuring dark wood panels, velvet sofas and silk drapes. The lingerie itself wasn't the often dull but practical everyday underwear that dominated the market – it tended towards frivolous and often completely impractical pieces fit only for a wedding night or burlesque show.

The first store opened in Stanford Shopping Center in Palo Alto, California, in 1977 and proved a reasonable success, returning a first-year profit of $500,000. Raymond opened more stores and launched a catalogue.

And everyone lived and dressed happily ever after.

Well, not entirely. The brand faltered, was sold and was ultimately re-launched … but that's another story for another time.

SPARKPOINT: *Researching your market before you try and enter it can provide valuable lessons, even if you go on to break what appear to be the established rules.*

6. THE LESSER-KNOWN SOURCES OF INSPIRATION – FORGETFULNESS AND EMBARRASSMENT

Words normally associated with innovation are creativity, originality and imagination. However, for businessman Frank McNamara, the words might be forgetfulness and embarrassment.

In the fall of 1949 Frank had taken some clients to dinner at Major's Cabin Grill, a restaurant in New York City. The meal came to an end and Frank asked for the bill, but when he reached into his jacket he was embarrassed to discover that he had forgotten his wallet.

Luckily for him, his wife was able to bail him out and he was saved from a long evening of washing dishes.

As the embarrassment faded he resolved never to be caught short like that again, and the germ of an idea came to him. He wondered why a businessman couldn't be free to spend what he could afford rather than how much cash he had in his pocket at the time.

He discussed his idea first with the restaurant owner and later with his lawyer and friend Ralph Schneider. Together they built the concept of a club of diners who would be able to sign for their suppers at selected restaurants and settle the bill at a later date.

Frank and Ralph formally founded Diners Club International on 8 February 1950 with $1.5 million of initial capital. Membership was $3 and Frank quickly recruited 200 friends and acquaintances as well as signing up 27 restaurants.

The pair decided they should celebrate the launch of their new venture and, of course, there was really only one way to do that. They returned to Major's Cabin and when the bill arrived Frank presented the owner with a small cardboard card, his Diners Club Card. It was an event that's now known as 'The First Supper'.

The Diners Club was an immediate hit. By year's end, 20,000 people were members. In 1952, franchises were established in Canada, Cuba and France. In 1955, Western Airlines became the first air carrier to accept the card for payment. In 1963 Danny Kaye starred in a movie, *The Man from the Diners Club*, in which he played an employee who issues a credit card to a well-known mobster and then has to retrieve it in order to keep his job.

SPARKPOINT: *Though a bit of a marketing cliché, a problem isn't always a problem – sometimes it can be an opportunity.*

7. NOT AN OVERNIGHT SENSATION

The accepted norm for stellar internet-based brands seems to be that it all starts with a couple of college mates who have a flash of inspiration – an idea that will engage and better the world.

They set up a website that becomes an overnight sensation, quickly leading to world domination.

Somehow reality isn't always quite like that.

Joe Gebbia and Brian Chesky fit the mould, in so far as they met in 2002 at the Rhode Island School of Design.

Joe had form when it came to entrepreneurship. He had designed a cushion for back pain sufferers, and had built a website where product designers could find eco-friendly resources, which he pitched as a 'sort of Amazon for sustainable materials'. Unfortunately, neither was very successful – certainly not on an Amazon-ian scale!

Meanwhile, Brian had recently left his job as a designer on a Simon Cowell television show, *American Inventor in LA*. As he put it, "The last straw came when I designed a new kind of toilet seat." He moved to San Francisco to share a flat with his old classmate Joe.

By 2007 the two were struggling to pay their rent. They needed some cash and they needed it fast. Their need coincided with an upcoming design conference in San Francisco, but rather than try and sell their design skills to the event organizers, they noticed that the city's hotels were fully booked … and that gave them an idea.

It was not an idea to better the world but to earn them their rent.

Could they rent out the space in their flat to people attending the conference?

They bought three airbeds, decided to sweeten the offer with the promise of breakfast and created the not very originally named *airbedandbreakfast.com* website. The cost was $80 a night. Six days later they had their first customers – a 30-year-old man from India, a 35-year-old woman from Boston and a 45-year-old father of four from Utah – sleeping on their floor.

Wondering if this could be something bigger, they got together with their old roommate and programming expert, Nathan Blecharczyk, to try and build a business.

For the first four months they worked on a roommate-matching service, until they realized that *roommates.com* already existed, at which point they went back to working on Air Bed and Breakfast.

They launched the brand for a second time, but no one noticed.

The third time, they decided to target a time and place when the local hotels should be full. It was the 2008 South by Southwest (SXSW) music festival in Austin, Texas, but they only managed to house two customers, and one of those was Brian. Perhaps not too surprisingly their attempts to raise capital weren't going well either. They approached 15 angel investors and got eight rejections; the other seven ignored them completely.

Still persevering, they tried again. Presidential nominee Barack Obama was due to speak at the Democratic National Convention in Denver, and 80,000 people were expected to be there. Once again, there was likely to be a shortage of hotel rooms.

Joe, Brian and Nathan launched a new website two weeks before the political convention. Within a week they had 800 listings, and on paper everything was looking good. However, given their costs, it looked like even with these 800 listings they weren't going to make any money.

Luckily, a PR stunt would come to their rescue.

In preparation for convention week, they had bought bulk quantities of breakfast cereal and designed packaging branded as *Obama's O's* and *Cap'n McCain* (after Republican nominee John McCain). They sold 800 'limited-edition' boxes at $40 each and made more than $30,000.

This got the attention of a venture capitalist named Paul Graham. Paul invited them to join Y Combinator, a prestigious start-up accelerator that provides cash and training in exchange for a small slice of a fledgling company. The team then spent the first three months of 2009 at the accelerator, working on further improving their offering.

Their lack of success with other VCs continued, and looking back, Fred Wilson of Union Square Ventures admitted to one of those 'guitar music is on the way out' moments. "We couldn't wrap our heads around air mattresses on the living room floors as the next hotel room, and we did not chase the deal," Fred said. "Others saw the amazing team that we saw, funded them, and the rest is history."

One thing that did change (perhaps because of feedback like Fred's) was that in March 2009 they dropped the Air Bed & Breakfast name, adopting the simplified 'Airbnb' to avoid further association with air mattresses.

One month later, Airbnb picked up a $600,000 seed investment from Sequoia Capital and from there the brand really began to take off.

> **SPARKPOINT:** *Innovation can take inspiration, perspiration and perseverance.*

8. THE BRAND THAT WENT DOWN THE DRAIN

Newcastle may not be the first place you think of as a centre of innovation, but this story will be the fourth one I've written about brands that were born in that northern English city.

Having written about Lucozade, Greggs and Newcastle Brown Ale, this brand story starts with a dentist before it literally goes down the drain.

Wilfred (sometimes spelt Wilfrid) Augustine Handley followed in his father's footsteps, and in the early 1900s became a dentist (or rather what at the time was called a 'dental mechanic'). Father and son practiced at the family home at 309 Chillingham Road for many years.

Wilfred's big idea started with what was a waste product, sodium hypochlorite. He bought it from the ICI chemical works at Billingham and used the compound as a bleaching agent to whiten dentures, and perhaps even intact teeth.

Wilfred knew the whitening solution had wider potential and started to dilute and bottle it.

In fact, bleach in one form or another had been around since the 18th century. In the late 19th century, E S Smith patented the chloralkali process for producing sodium hypochlorite, which was initially sold as a bleach under a number of brand names, none of which met with great success.

While Wilfred didn't actually invent bleach, he did get the marketing and distribution right.

First, he chose a brand name. According to the brand's current owner, Unilever, he chose a combination of the Latin 'domus', meaning house, and the Greek 'osteon', meaning bone, suggesting the 'backbone of the home'.

Wilfred's family tell it a little differently. An alternative version holds that the dentist-entrepreneur asked his mother what his product should be called. Before answering, she asked what it was for. When Wilfred replied, 'Domestic use', she came up with 'Domestos'.

Similarly, his second innovation was not a completely original idea either – it was probably inspired by the success of another local brand, Ringtons Tea, which had been established in the Liverpool suburb of Heaton in 1907. Ringtons was sold door-to-door in the area, with great success, and that was what Wilfred decided to do as well.

He bottled Domestos bleach in large brown earthenware jars, which then could be refilled by door-to-door salesmen pushing hand carts or riding bicycle carts.

The bleach was promoted as a cleaning agent to whiten linens and white clothing and to pour down drains to 'sweeten' them. It was a real success. By 1933, Wilfred's goods were being shipped south to Hull by sea. and within two years supply depots had opened in both Hull and Middlesbrough.

The brand prospered during World War II when it was more broadly marketed as a cure for sore feet and a treatment for burns.

The war's end could have slowed things down, as the company was unable to acquire enough delivery vehicles. Showing more ingenuity, Domestos overcame the problem by purchasing the St Ann's Works at Heaton Junction and setting up their own coach-building division. By 1952 there was national distribution, with offices in London, Manchester, Cardiff, York and Glasgow, as well as a national research laboratory.

In 1961, Wilfred sold the brand to Lever Brothers Ltd.

SPARKPOINT: *If the right supply chain isn't there, or the current one isn't serving your purpose, you may need to be brave enough to do it yourself.*

9. FROM BOOKS TO BEAUTY AND THE FIRST AVON LADY (WHO WAS ACTUALLY A MAN)

Despite its name being inspired by the British river, Avon's origins are American. The business actually started in books, not beauty, and the first 'Avon Lady' was in fact a man.

That first Avon 'Lady' was a young door-to-door salesman, David McConnell, who originally came from Oswego, New York. He began working for the Union

Publishing Company in 1877, selling magazines, greeting cards and books. He was reasonably successful and purchased 50% of the company for $500.

David found that books weren't always an easy sell, and he resorted to the then-popular marketing ploy of offering a free introductory gift in exchange for being allowed to come in and make his sales pitch.

Given that most of his clients were women, he thought a complimentary vial of perfume would work well. So, with some help from a local pharmacist, David blended the original scent himself. He soon discovered that many of his customers were much more interested in the fragrance than they were in his books.

"The book business was not congenial to me," he would later say. And so he announced to his business partner, who had now moved to California, his intention to sell perfume. His partner enthusiastically agreed and even suggested that he call the new company the California Perfume Company, "because of the great profusion of flowers in California."

The door-to-door formula for perfume sales was ideal for that time period in America. David focused on small towns, where his home-based clients often had no means of travelling to shops where they could buy things like perfume. As his biography characterized it: "At the turn of the century, about 80% of the California Perfume Company's 'Depot Agents' lived and sold in communities of less than 1,000 (white) population."

However, what really took the brand to new heights was when David realized that the perfect salesperson might in fact be a woman. He hired his first female sales representative – the first 'Avon Lady' – Persis Foster

Eames Albee, a 50-year-old wife and mother of two. McConnell would later call her the 'Mother of the California Perfume Company'.

It is she who is credited with creating the company's system for distributing products. Persis travelled around the American northeast by buggy and train, not only selling door-to-door herself but recruiting and training other women as salespeople. She recognized that these agents wouldn't necessarily have to travel, but could sell in their own communities. The fact they were actually part of the communities in which they sold gave them credibility with their friends and neighbours, a level of trustworthiness and accessibility that no travelling salesman could match.

The company allowed these women to purchase products and literature and resell the items in their own time and in their own style. It was the first time this kind of approach had been used in cosmetics and it helped the brand prosper for over a century.

What Persis and David were now selling was a business opportunity for women – usually older, married women who needed money. It would give them the chance to earn an independent income. It was an appealing idea, and in 1887, just one year into their perfume business, they already had a team of 12 agents selling an 18-product fragrance line.

In 1905 the company launched *Outlook* magazine, a publication for sharing advice with employees and keeping representatives up-to-date on other company news. The following year they had enough products to release a sales catalogue, another move that helped drive sales.

It wasn't until 1928 that the company started using the Avon name. Different sources say it came from the fact that it was the birthplace of Shakespeare, David's favourite playwright, or that when visiting the bard's home in Stratford-upon-Avon he was taken by how the countryside resembled that around his home in rural upstate New York.

The name may have changed and the product range expanded, but the brand remains committed to empowering women around the globe. In fact, its stated purpose is 'to create a world with more empowered women'. It aims to stay true to the set of guiding principles that David espoused all those years ago:

- Providing an earning opportunity so individuals can achieve financial independence and enjoy all that comes with such an accomplishment.
- Recognizing everyone's unique contributions.
- Giving back to the communities Avon serves.
- Offering the highest quality products with a guarantee of satisfaction.
- Maintaining and cherishing the 'friendly spirit of Avon'.

The moral of the story is that it isn't just what you sell but the way that you sell it.

Is there a better route to market for your brand?

SPARKPOINT: *Innovation needs you to think not only about who you are going to sell to, but how and by whom that selling should be done.*

Footnote: Avon is not the only brand where the founder started in one business but realized that his 'door opener' gift would prove to be the truly successful brand. William Wrigley Jr sold soap and baking powder, giving away sticks of chewing gum, before moving into the confectionery business.

10. FROM WASTED TO WANTED, DOING WHAT THEY SAID COULDN'T BE DONE

Over the years I've worked on many different brands, from lots of different categories and in a variety of different countries.

One of the brands I feel very lucky to have worked on in recent years is E-Leather.

They describe themselves on their website as 'an award winning, environmentally friendly materials technology company that uses traditional leather fibres and high-powered water to produce a technologically advanced eco-leather material'.

However, that doesn't do them justice.

On an early visit to their site, I noticed a tribute to their founder, the late inventor Chris Bevan. It read:

Somebody said that it "couldn't be done ..."
But, he with a chuckle replied that "maybe it couldn't,"
but he would be one who wouldn't say so till he'd tried.
So he buckled right in with the trace of a grin on his face.
If he worried he hid it.
He started to sing as he tackled
the thing that couldn't be done,
and he did it.

Somebody scoffed: "Oh, you'll never do that;
at least no one has done it";
but he took off his coat and he took off his hat,
and the first thing we knew he'd begun it.
With a lift of his chin and a bit of a grin,
without any doubting or quiddit,
he started to sing as he tackled
the thing that couldn't be done,
and he did it.

There are thousands to tell you it cannot be done,
there are thousands to prophesy failure;
there are thousands to point out to you one by one,
the dangers that wait to assail you.
But just buckle it in with a bit of a grin,
just take off your coat and go to it;
just start to sing as you tackle
the thing that "couldn't be done,"
and you'll do it.

It turns out that Chris was a man who hated unnecessary waste. When he learned that up to 50% of leather hides end up in the landfill, he decided that something needed to be done.

His first idea was to use the leather offcuts (scraps) from the shoe industry and turn them into insulation. The idea wasn't so much recycling as *upcycling*. The offcuts hadn't been used but they were still being treated as waste. His idea was to upgrade the wasted into something wanted.

Creating a viable insulation product proved difficult, as the fibres would often clog up before forming into the desired blocks, but that didn't stop Chris.

Some versions of the story have new inspiration following a fall. One day, still looking for a solution, Chris reportedly slipped on a bit of shredded leather in the lab and fell into a heap of it. Getting up, he noticed how the fibres had been compressed together into what looked like a new mini-sheet of leather. It gave him an idea – rather than trying to fabricate insulation, he started to think about how he could create something altogether different.

I've been told that the story of this fall is just that, a story. However, Chris' determination was genuine, and he did finally find an alternative use for the unwanted offcuts, which was an entirely new material.

Using what is a now patented technology and based on the wonderfully named 'hydro-entanglement' process, Chris found a way to sandwich genuine leather fibres around a micro textile inner core, all without the use of any adhesives, to create a leather-fibre composite that was christened E-Leather. It is a high-tech, high-performance material that contains a high percentage of real leather, but it's much lighter and more economical than traditional leather.

While it looks and feels just like leather, it can be produced in rolls, something that can't be done with traditional leather. This means E-Leather is easier to use, considerably reducing manufacturing waste.

The company's initial products were introduced in 2007 and the business has grown from an original niche in aviation to include product lines for ground transport, commercial and domestic furniture, and footwear. Production and sales have grown rapidly and the company has won numerous 'green' awards along the way.

Not bad for something they said couldn't be done.

Chris died in 2012, but as the company says in its publicity materials, it "still honours the vision of our founder Chris Bevan, and his commitment to the development of a clean technology product and culture."

For me what makes this brand so special is how it cleverly turns the wasted into the wanted, with a wonderful trinity of benefits – it is a product that is good for businesses, good for customers and good for the planet.

SPARKPOINT: *One person's waste can be another's inspiration; try to look at things from different perspectives and find new uses.*

11. A SECOND 'EUREKA' MOMENT – BATH TIME INSPIRATION

John Adrian Shepherd-Barron was letting off steam while sitting in steam.

It was 1965 and banks kept strict business hours. John had failed to get to his branch on time to withdraw the money he needed for the upcoming weekend, and still fuming he had returned home and decided to take a bath.

Ensconced in his tub, like Archimedes he had a 'eureka' moment. "It struck me there must be a way I could get my own money, anywhere in the world," he later recalled.

"I hit upon the idea of a chocolate bar dispenser, but replacing chocolate with cash."

Luckily for him, his work at De La Rue Instruments – a British banknote manufacturer, security printer and paper maker – provided an opportunity to meet the chief general manager of Barclays Bank on other matters. John grabbed the opportunity to pitch his idea: "If you put your standard Barclays cheque through a slot in the side of the bank," he said, the cash-dispensing machine would "deliver standard amounts of money around the clock."

A contract was quickly drawn up and signed, over a pink gin cocktail according to some versions of the story. Yet, it wouldn't be until 1967 that the world's first automated teller machine (ATM) would be installed at a Barclays branch in the north London suburb of Enfield.

Actor Reg Varney, from the television series *On the Buses*, was hired to be the first person to withdraw cash from this first ATM.

The machines worked with cheques, each of which had to be impregnated with a mildly radioactive chemical – fortunately it was one that was harmless to humans. The cheques were also encoded with a personal identification number (PIN) that the user had to key in.

It was John's wife who suggested that a four-digit code should be used, as she thought that six figures would be too many for most people to remember.

The first machines paid out only £10 but, as John observed at the time, this was "quite enough for a wild weekend."

SPARKPOINT: *What can you 'borrow' from another market and introduce into your market?*

12. THINK SIDEWAYS – DON'T LET YOUR THINKING BE CONSTRAINED

In my book *The Prisoner and the Penguin*, I told the story of how a banjo-playing, engineering school dropout and 3M employee named Dick Drew created masking tape.

Two-tone cars were all the rage in the 1920s, but they were causing a serious problem for mechanics in body shops as they tried to create this effect. The problem was masking – protecting adjoining, different-coloured areas when paint was applied.

No one knew how to do this well, so most improvised. They glued old newspapers to the body and windows with library pastes, home-made glues or surgical adhesive tape. While this helped create a sharp demarcation between the two colours, the adhesives stuck so firmly that trying to remove them often ruined the paint job.

As someone who relished a challenge, Dick vowed to solve the problem. He finally did so using ingenuity and a little bit of cheek to get around 3M's procurement gatekeepers and get his prototype made. The answer was in effect sandpaper without the sand, making it sticky enough but not utilizing a permanent adhesive.

This was the end of my masking tape innovation story, but in fact it's just a chapter in the metaphorical bigger 'book' of 3M innovations.

One of the next chapters features Dick again. Working on another project – and now technical director of 3M's Product Fabrication Laboratory in Minnesota – he was immediately intrigued when one of his team members showed him a sample of a new moisture-proof packaging material from Dupont. It was called Cellophane.

Dick saw its potential as a new backing for masking tape, and, despite having to reformulate the adhesive that would be used, he and his team went on to produce what was originally called Scotch Brand Cellulose Tape. It was later renamed Scotch Transparent Tape and is now known simply as Scotch Tape.

So ended another chapter, but 3M's innovation book continued to grow as Larry Wendling, the company's VP of Corporate Research, explained in *Imagine: How Creativity Works.**

"You might think an idea is finished, that there's nothing else to do with it, but then you talk to somebody else in some other field," he said. "And your little idea inspires them, so they come up with a brand-new invention that inspires someone else. That, in a nutshell, is our model."

The innovation trail that produced masking tape led the researchers' thinking into panelling and then sound dampening panels. Innovation in those areas was based on the adhesives used in industrial strength masking tape. This, in turn, led to the development of another product for another market – Scotch-Weld, a super-strong adhesive foam.

The adhesive from Scotch Tape was the basis for many of 3M's inventions, including smart screen technology, coatings and specialist light refracting films.

As Larry aptly concludes, "The lesson is that the tape business isn't just about tape."

SPARKPOINT: *One innovation can lead to another, so look for ways in which you can further innovate on your original innovation.*

* Jonah Lehrer, *Imagine: How Creativity Works*, Houghton Mifflin Harcourt (19 March 2012), page 41.

13. IN SPITE OF, NOT BECAUSE OF

Today Coca-Cola is undoubtedly one of the world's greatest brands, successful in hundreds of countries. It wasn't however always like that.

Up until the late 1930s, Coca-Cola's only real international success was in Germany, where sales records were being set and beaten year after year. By 1939 Coca-Cola had 43 bottling plants and more than 600 local distributors there. However, storm clouds – and even worse, Stormtroopers – were massing.

As World War II began a trade embargo was imposed, which put a halt to the supply of key ingredients necessary for the production of Coca-Cola syrup.

To further complicate matters, the man who had been in charge of Coca-Cola's operations in Germany, American-born Ray Powers, died of injuries received in an automobile accident in 1938.

German-born Max Keith took over. He was committed to keeping production going and keeping people employed. He decided to try and create a new product but knew that they would only be able to get what he later called the 'leftovers of leftovers'. And so, he and his team used whey and apple pomace – the skins, pulp, seeds and stems of fruit that had already been pressed – to concoct a light-coloured drink that resembled ginger ale.

The new product needed a name, and so Max called together some employees for a competition. He told them to let their *fantasie* (man for fantasy) run wild. Upon hearing that, veteran salesman Joe Knipp immediately suggested 'Fanta'.

Fanta was a success, despite the fact that its flavour varied depending on what fruits and other leftovers were available. In its earliest incarnations, the drink was sweetened with saccharin, but by 1941 Max and his team were allowed to use 3.5% beet sugar in their recipes. In 1943 some three million cases of Fanta were sold, which was enough to keep the German plants operating and Coca-Cola staff employed.

While all this was happening, executives at Coca-Cola in Atlanta – who had had no contact with their German affiliate throughout World War II – did not know if Max was still working for the company or for the Nazis. Communication with him had been impossible.

So, after the war, an investigator was commissioned by Coca-Cola to examine Max's actions. The American executives were delighted to hear that Max had not only never been a Nazi, he'd repeatedly rebuffed pressure to become one and suffered hardships because of those refusals. He had also resisted the temptation to sell Fanta under his own name.

It is now recognized that it was largely thanks to Max's efforts that Coca-Cola was able to re-establish production in Germany almost immediately after World War II.

As for Fanta, it was discontinued, but as competition in new flavours increased in the 1950s, it was relaunched in 1955.

Nowadays, while orange is the main Fanta variety, the soft drink is sold in more than 100 flavours worldwide.

SPARKPOINT: *Sometimes necessity can be the mother of invention, and putting someone in a difficult situation can actually fire their imagination.*

14. THEY WILL NEVER SELL

Dick Rowe of Decca Records is (in)famously reported to have said, "Guitar groups are on their way out, Mr Epstein," in turning down the Beatles in 1962.

To date, the Beatles have sold more than 600 million albums worldwide.

Similarly, as the British government was looking for an automobile for the masses after World War II, it turned down the Volkswagen Beetle, saying: "This car does not fulfil the technical requirements which must be expected from a motor car. Its performance and qualities have no attraction to the average buyer. It is too ugly and too noisy."

More than 21.5 million of the iconic old VW 'Bugs' had been sold when the last one rolled off the production line in Mexico in 2003.

When Nathan Clark presented the design for a new boot, his board of directors felt it was too informal and not in line with their traditional designs. Their verdict: "They will never sell."

In 1941, Nathan was stationed in Burma with the British Army. As the great-grandson of one of the founders of the Clarks Company, it wasn't surprising that he paid particular attention to what people were wearing on their feet. He soon noticed that many off-duty officers were wearing simple suede boots with crepe soles.

Investigating further, he found out that the officers were ordering their boots from a particular bazaar in Cairo. They were made to be lightweight (so they were easier to run in), had a grippy sole (for balance on any type of ground) and the suede upper was both comfortable and good in high temperatures.

Believing he was onto something big, he began cutting prototype patterns out of newsprint. He sent these clippings along with drawings back home to the factory, in the village of Street in Somerset.

When he got back to England, Nathan sourced the finest materials and found some shoemakers to transform his idea into reality. Using an existing last (a three-dimensional mould upon which a shoe is constructed) that had been used for a popular Clarks sandal, he began to experiment. He used what is known as a stitch-down construction, a method used in other Clarks styles, but opted for an orange thread as a further distinguishing trait.

Sticking to the look he had seen in Burma, he decided on a beige suede, sourcing it from a nearby tannery, Charles F Stead. The colour of the suede was a reference to the boot's desert origins, however, the material was to prove more controversial as most men's shoes at the time were made from stiff, formal, dark leather.

Presenting his unconventional Desert Boot prototype to the board, he was met with a frosty response – in short, they thought the shoes would never sell.

Nathan, however, still believed in his new boot, so in his capacity as the company's Overseas Development Manager he unilaterally decided to take his latest creation to the Chicago Shoe Fair in 1949.

It was well received, and was dubbed the world's first 'dress casual' shoe.

So, in 1950 the Clarks Desert Boot finally went on sale. It was an immediate success.

More than 10 million pairs of what was described in a 1957 advert as 'the world's most travelled shoes' have been sold in 100 countries.

Famous fans have included Steve McQueen, Bob Dylan, Robbie Williams, cabinet minister Kenneth Clarke and even *Sex and the City* actress Sarah Jessica Parker, who was spotted buying two pairs – one in brown, one in black – because she couldn't decide which she liked best.

Rock star Liam Gallagher of the band Oasis was such a fan that throughout the 1990s he hardly wore anything else. He went one step further and collaborated with Clarks to design his own version of the boot as part of his 'Pretty Green' clothing label.

The boot was named one of the 'Fifty Shoes That Changed the World' by the UK's Design Museum in 2009.

SPARKPOINT: *Innovations need support – they need people who believe in them and will advocate and fight for them, even in the face of resistance.*

15. LOVE ME, LOVE MY DOG – ZAPPOS ON STEROIDS

Zappos, the online shoe and clothing retailer, is almost universally held up in the marketing world as the benchmark when it comes to customer experience. So how could a brand ever expect to become *Zappos on steroids*?

Well, our story begins in failure, as do so many success stories.

In 2011, Ryan Cohen and his business partner Michael Day had to finally admit that their budding online jewellery site was going nowhere … and fast. They sold their entire remaining inventory at a loss, but rather than just give up they decided to try again.

Reflecting on why the jewellery site had failed, they recognized that, in Ryan's words, "We're not passionate about what we're doing."

This got them thinking about what they were truly passionate about. For Ryan it was obvious – it was his poodle, Tylee. He knew he was a dedicated 'pet parent', someone who would happily spend on premium food and other products for their dog.

From there it wasn't hard to flesh out the idea: there must be lots of other pet parents who were willing to spend lots on the very best products. A quick review of the market confirmed that there was a gap. "So," Ryan said, "I was going to the pet store and realized the market online was really under-penetrated. This was a much better opportunity."

Ryan and Michael took their thinking a step further and concluded that not only would these pet parents appreciate good products, they would probably want great service from like-minded people. "From the beginning," Ryan said, "we came in saying that we want to provide pet parents with the most amazing customer experience. Period. Zappos on steroids."

And so, they retooled their jewellery site into Chewy. com. The food and accessories they offered on their website weren't really different from what pet owners could buy in stores, so the difference was in the service.

While the two founders originally answered customer calls themselves, they soon needed to hire some extra help. They wanted exactly the right type of people, people they now call *Chewtopians* – 'Pet-loving, adventure-seeking, silly-hat-wearing folks whose sole mission is to enrich the bond between you and your pets'.

As with all things in service, it is actions and not words that really make the difference, and Ryan, Michael and their Chewtopians acted differently.

Perhaps the most famous example of the brand living up to their ideals is the story of Dallas, Texas, resident Sheree Flanagan, which was initially published in *People Magazine.*

On 22 December 2016, Sheree's much-loved dog, Zoe, died and the bereaved pet parent spent the holidays trying to come to terms with her loss.

Then tragedy struck again on 30 January, when Thor, her 15-year-old cat, died.

"Losing Zoe was terrible," said Sheree. "We had her for ten years, but when Thor died that was crushing. He lived with me in New York, then California and now here. He was always my No. 1 boy."

Trying hard to be practical, Sheree called the Chewy customer service number to see if she could return her unused pet food.

She was put through to a Chewtopian named Ashley. "Ashley was amazing," Sheree said. "She told me she had a cat put down and she really understood. I kept saying that I didn't mean to bother her and she kept saying, 'No, this is important. Tell me more.'"

As you might expect from a brand dedicated to good service, Sheree got a full refund, and no documentation was asked for.

What happened next exemplified Chewy's difference in action. The following day a van pulled up at Sheree's home. It was there to deliver a bouquet of flowers and a note of condolence. It read, "With deepest sympathy on your loss of your little ones. We'll always be here through the sad times and to remember the good memories your fur babies left on your heart. Love – Ashley and the Chewy Family."

This isn't a one-off, but is part of that ultimate customer service the brand is dedicated to. There are numerous similar stories online.

Kelli Durkin, Chewy's VP of customer service, says of their focus on the customer: "We don't feel we're talking to customers. We are talking to pet parents. We want to hear the good and the bad. We are feeding their children. We are part of their families."

The company's personalized service is based on the principle of 'zero automation' in the customer service department – some 450 representatives operate the centre, 24/7, 365 days a year, answering calls in just 4-6 seconds.

The brand has a 'WOW' department that sends out the bereavement packages, cards and more to customers who experience life events ranging from illnesses to weddings. It donates a portion of its profits to no-kill animal shelters.

All customers get entered into a lottery to win one of 700 weekly hand-made oil paintings of their pet (Chewy now has 200 full-time portrait artists). The company also has a 40-strong TV crew with three sound stages producing pet-care tutorials for the Chewy YouTube channel.

Not surprisingly, Chewy's sales have grown exponentially, from $26 million in 2012 to $900 million in 2016. The company went on to book $2 billion in revenue in 2017, accounting for over 50% of the online pet food market.

SPARKPOINT: *Turning your passion into your purpose can be a source of inspiration.*

Footnote: In 2017 the pet industry giant PetSmart bought Chewy for $3.35 billion, one of the largest e-commerce acquisitions ever.

16. THE WASP

"It looks like a wasp!"

Not quite the endorsement that Corradino D'Ascanio was expecting when he presented the fruits of his hard work to his patron.

Yet within months the Italian language possessed a new verb based on the brand.

To date over 16 million of Corradino's products have been sold around the world and they're produced in 13 countries.

They have become a screen icon starring alongside Audrey Hepburn in *Roman Holiday*, Anita Ekberg in *La Dolce Vita*, Angie Dickinson in *Jessica* and Gwen Stefani in her 2007 video for the song *Now That You Got It*.

If you still haven't figured out the brand yet, it also appeared in 1979 film *Quadrophenia*, where Sting and every other Mod who could afford one was riding one.

The brand is, of course, Vespa.

Following the end of World War II, industrialist Enrico Piaggio needed to find a new direction for his company, which had been making planes for the Italian Air Force. He recognized that Italy had an urgent need for a modern and affordable mode of transport. And so, he tasked Corradino, one of his aeronautical engineers, with designing a motorcycle suitable for getting around bomb-damaged Italian cities.

However, Corradino wasn't keen on motorcycles. He thought they were too cumbersome, too difficult to repair and generally dirty.

Instead, he took inspiration from having seen US military aircraft drop tiny, olive-green Cushman Airbornes to their troops in the war-torn cities of Milan and Turin. The Cushman Airborne was a basic, skeletal, steel motor scooter that allowed troops to nip about the rough terrain.

Adapting his aeronautical expertise to the task in hand, Corradino designed a simple but practical scooter. He moved the gear lever onto the handlebar for easier access. He designed the body to absorb stress in the same way as an aircraft would. The seat was positioned to provide both safety and comfort, the workings were hidden behind panels to keep the rider's clothes in pristine condition, and the step-through frame meant it was an ideal machine for skirt-wearing women to ride.

In fact, the first Vespas actually used components from Enrico's aircraft, including the nose wheel suspension for the scooter's front wheel.

It was ultimately the vehicle's narrow-waisted design and buzzing sound that caused Enrico to exclaim, "Sembra una vespa!" ("It looks like a wasp!") With that spontaneous reaction, the scooter had its brand name.

In April 1946 the Vespa debuted at a golf club in Rome, and it was an immediate success. It wasn't long before 'vespare' (to go somewhere on a Vespa) was being heard on the streets, along with the wasp-like buzzing of the scooters' engines.

SPARKPOINT: *Technical expertise can be transferred into other new sectors. Where could your technical expertise be used to good effect?*

17. THE IDEAL HUSBAND – HOW TO WIN A WOMAN'S HEART WITH A BOWL OF CUSTARD

Next Valentine's Day, what are you planning for your special one?

A card at least, I hope, but maybe a bunch of flowers, a bottle of champagne or a romantic dinner for two?

But how would your partner react if you gave them a bowl of custard? Yes, custard – that sweet, yellow dessert sauce we Brits pour over our rhubarb crumble and apple pies.

Well, if you were Mrs Elizabeth Bird you would be delighted.

Now the exact date in 1837 on which Alfred Bird presented a bowl of custard to his wife is not known, but whenever it was it clearly won him some serious brownie points.

Elizabeth had persistent digestive problems and suffered severe reactions to eggs and yeast-based products. But she was a lover of custard, and despite the consequences she simply couldn't resist the stuff.

Alfred had qualified as a Fellow of the Chemists Society and set up a shop in Birmingham's Bell Street, selling household medicines and toiletries. Business was good, but Alfred wasn't satisfied, and every night after the shop closed he indulged his passion for experimental chemistry. The task he set himself was to find a way to help his wife enjoy the foods she loved.

He began a quest for an egg-free custard and finally, after many late nights, he developed a recipe for a new custard powder based on corn flour.

His wife was delighted, and soon too were some friends of the Birds', when they were introduced to the confection by mistake.

The story goes that it was 'accidentally' fed to some of Elizabeth and Alfred's guests at a dinner party. Seeing their reaction, Alfred realized that perhaps there was more to his invention than just a happier wife.

Bird's Powdered Custard was born, and lives on successfully to this day.

A few years later Alfred again proved what an ideal husband he was, when in 1843 he came up with a yeast substitute. It was originally called 'Bird's Fermenting

Powder' but was quickly renamed 'Baking Powder'. It not only helped people like Elizabeth, who had yeast allergies, but was soon widely used to help people bake lighter bread, cakes and pastries.

It was, and is still, a success.

> **SPARKPOINT:** *Solving someone's problem*
> *(loved one or not) is a well-used*
> *path to innovation.*

18. GO WEST YOUNG MAN ... AND MOISTURIZE

Seeing what other cannot see, risking your life savings and self-inflicting cuts and burns – have you got what it takes to be an innovator?

Robert Chesebrough had.

Robert was a British chemist who worked at distilling the oil from sperm whales into lighting fuel, but recognized that time was running out for whale oil. The future, he realized, lay in petroleum.

So, he used his life savings and like other young men in the mid-19th century he 'went west', buying a ticket to the US and ending up in Titusville, Pennsylvania.

One day, while touring one of the oil fields there, he noticed a rigger scraping a thick, dark goo from an oil pump's joint. He asked what it was.

At first, it sounded like just an unwanted and potentially hazardous by-product. The wax-like gunk tended to come up with the crude oil and would collect on the rigging. If it wasn't cleaned off regularly, it would gum up the works. The riggers called it 'rod wax'.

However, the workmen went on to tell Robert that many of them used the waxy substance on cuts and burns because it helped them heal quicker.

Robert was intrigued and he saw what might be a big opportunity. Rod wax was an unvalued by-product – something that was thrown away – and if he could turn into something with real value, the potential profit margin was going to be enormous.

He easily persuaded the riggers to let him have some of the wax and took it away to start experimenting.

It would take him several years, but in the end he discovered that by distilling lighter, thinner oil from the rod wax, he could create a light-coloured gel. His process, which he'd eventually patent, involved vacuum distillation of the crude material followed by filtration of the still residue through bone char.

Now all he had to do was persuade people that it was worth having.

Robert started travelling around New York selling his Vaseline, a name that combined the German word for water (*wasser*) and the Greek word for oil (*elaion*).

Being odourless and colourless meant that it had obvious benefits over animal- and plant-derived alternatives like lard, goose grease, olive oil and garlic oil, which were often rank and smelly, but he needed to show that it actually worked.

As part of his sales pitch, he literally started using himself as a guinea pig. He'd cut himself or burn his skin with acid or an open flame, and then spread the ointment on his injuries. He'd also show how well his past injuries had healed with the help of his miracle salve.

People were convinced and started to buy the product. Soon pharmacists were asking to stock it, and in 1870 Robert opened his first factory, doing business as the Chesebrough Manufacturing Company (later Chesebrough-Ponds).

While it is still used for cuts and burns, Vaseline is also regularly used on dry and unruly hair, and in ways that Robert could never have imagined. For instance, it's used on the feet of vending machines to keep pests out and some farmers are known to put it on chickens to prevent frostbite.

SPARKPOINT: *Not all ideas will come fully formed, so look at things from different perspectives, and be on the lookout for the germ of a new idea. Can you find a behaviour that is established but where the product isn't obvious?*

19. BEAM ME UP AN INNOVATION

Marketers are often asked to come up with the next big thing, but looking into the future isn't always easy.

One way I've got around this is to 'ask' someone who is better at predicting things than I am – namely, a science fiction writer. And who better than Gene Roddenberry, the creator of the original *Star Trek* television series?

Michael Cooper is another innovator who drew his inspiration from the same source. After serving in the US Navy, Michael received a degree in electrical engineering from the Illinois Institute of Technology and then joined Motorola, where he worked on pagers and then car phones using cellular technology. At this point in time, car phones were 'mobile phones' only in the sense that they moved when the car did.

By the early 1970s Michael was getting worried that Motorola's great rival, AT&T, was gaining a lead in car phone technology.

One night he was watching *Star Trek*, one of his favourite TV shows, when inspiration struck. Seeing Captain James T Kirk using his communicator to call the Starship Enterprise, he had an idea. Could they develop a handheld mobile phone and leapfrog AT&T?

From that moment of inspiration, Michael and his team took only 90 days to create and build the portable cellular 800 MHz phone prototype.

On 3 April 1973, in front of a group of journalists on Sixth Avenue in New York City, Michael made the first public phone call from their prototype handheld cellular phone.

Who did he call?

His wife?

His mother?

His workmates?

No, he decided that it was too good an opportunity to miss and decided to call Joel Engel.

Joel was the head of research at AT&T Bell Labs and Michael called to tell him all about their new invention.

"As I walked down the street while talking on the phone, sophisticated New Yorkers gaped at the sight of someone actually moving around while making a phone call," Michael said. "Remember that in 1973, there weren't cordless telephones, let alone cellular phones. I made numerous calls, including one where I crossed the street while talking to a New York radio reporter – probably one of the more dangerous things I have ever done in my life."

SPARKPOINT: *Watching TV, especially if it's a sci-fi series or movie, can be a source of inspiration for future applications of technology.*

20. TOASTING THE TOWER

The drink most associated with the celebratory launch of something is champagne, so you would expect that the opening of the Eiffel Tower would have been toasted with a glass of the bubbly stuff from the northeast of France.

You would, however, only be half right.

On the night of 31 March 1899, when the tower was opened as one of the temporary exhibits of the Universal Exhibition, only one drink was served – a cocktail of champagne and Courvoisier cognac. Courvoisier went on to be awarded a Gold Medal at the exhibition and the tower proved so popular it became a permanent feature on the Parisian skyline.

Courvoisier was, and still is, immensely popular in France. It is linked with other key moments and figures of French history, but one in particular stands out.

The brand had been established in the Parisian suburb of Bercy in 1809, by Emmanuel Courvoisier and Louis Gallois, the mayor of Bercy. The business began life as a wine and spirits company, but Emmanuel and Louis' reputation quickly grew as purveyors of the very best cognacs. The pair decided that if they were going to build on this success, and to guarantee their supply of the finest cognacs, they should relocate to the brandy's home region itself and become producers.

In 1811, a famous fan visited the brand's new home and his visit was captured in a painting by Étienne Bouhot. The fan was none other than Napoleon Bonaparte.

So taken with the brand was he that he decided to order some for his artillery companies to lift their morale during the ongoing Napoleonic Wars. He told his commanders, "While you are on the march, [I] have issued to your forces, as much as may be possible, wine in the evening and cognac in the morning."

It seems cognac wasn't seen as just an after-dinner drink at the time.

Even after his defeat at the Battle of Waterloo, the liquor's connection to Napoleon continued. Exiled to the remote island of St Helena, in the Atlantic Ocean, legend has it that he was allowed to choose one item of luxury to take with him. It is said that he chose several casks of his beloved Courvoisier cognac and that one day, after dinner with English officers aboard HMS Northumberland, he treated them to a taste.

The officers loved it, and christened it 'The Brandy of Napoleon'.

The link remains and is commemorated in Courvoisier's logo, which features an outline drawing of the emperor.

I don't know whether the producers of the BBC Radio's *Desert Island Discs* programme – where hypothetical castaways are allowed to choose one item of luxury to carry into exile – borrowed the idea from the British Navy's courtesy to Napoleon. Neither do I know if anyone has actually chosen Courvoisier as their single wish-list luxury item.

What I do know is that I can thoroughly recommend the Courvoisier and champagne cocktail, though perhaps not first thing in the morning.

SPARKPOINT: *Can you land a celebrity endorsement of your innovation? It can help enormously.*

21. THE CURRY CYCLE, A STORY OF 'INDOVATION'

Manish Sharma is a man who recognizes that brands need to be the same but different. He advocates against a rigid belief in absolute brand consistency, and instead adheres to an understanding of the benefits of a looser concept of brand coherency.

Manish, the President & CEO of Panasonic India, wants to remain true to the company's global vision but at the same time recognizes that this has to be tailored for his market and its particular quirks.

"Our commitment at Panasonic is to provide a 'better life' for our consumers and contribute to creating a 'better world' around them," he said. "The requirement of our audience differs across geographies and therefore technological solutions have to be customized to the local environment. With this philosophy, we intend to provide solutions that are made in India for the Indians, across business and consumer sectors."

He continued: "India is at the cusp of change, and is being recognized as one of the most influential markets globally. Taking into account these unique local conditions, Panasonic is now looking at India as a priority market. Taking from our legacy, we will continue to provide solutions which will now be fuelled by our 'Indovation' strategy of weaving local solutions to our global approach."

Panasonic's new Stainmaster washing machine is one example of Indovation in action. Recently launched, it has a special wash cycle to tackle curry stains. Panasonic found that existing washing machines on the market failed to fully get food off clothes, which led to customer complaints and was slowing market growth.

Panasonic set out to solve the problem, looking at the specific stain-making ingredients in curries and testing hundreds of different combinations of water temperature and water flow. It took them two years to establish the optimal time and water temperature required to remove the stains.

Having identified and solved the curry problem, Panasonic also considered other tough, local cleaning challenges. So, in addition to the curry option, the machine has five other special cycles, including one to remove traces of hair oil.

Only about 10% of homes in India have a washing machine, with most people still doing their laundry by hand. South Korean manufacturers dominate the market, but Panasonic hopes its new settings will help to both grow the market and win the company market share, despite their machine carrying a 10% price premium.

It is currently winning the PR (and bad pun) battle with headlines about 'Spicing up the market' and 'Currying favour with Indian consumers'.

SPARKPOINT: *Local or regional innovation can be valuable as long as market potential is big enough.*

22. CAULIFLOWERS FOR TOURISTS – A FAIR EXCHANGE?

They say fair exchange is no robbery, and trading tons of cauliflowers for thousands of tourists seems to be a perfect example of the idiom. It was an exchange inspired by a visionary Breton, Alexis Gourvennec.

Alexis was a pig farmer who became an economic and social leader and would play a major role in the regeneration of France's Brittany region after World War II.

He led a group of Bretons who pressed the French administration with five key demands in the late 1960s. These included establishing a modern road network between the region and Paris, and the construction of a deep-water port at Roscoff.

In October 1968, the French government agreed to these demands.

However, Alexis wasn't finished. When Britain announced it would join the European Economic Community trading bloc, he saw an opportunity to open up a whole new export market for local cauliflowers, artichokes and other produce. Recognizing that the quickest route to this new market would be westward, across the English Channel to Plymouth, he contacted several large shipping companies to gauge their interest in operating the route. He was met with general scepticism.

Alexis and his group of Breton farmers didn't give up on their dream. They decided that if the established shipping companies wouldn't develop such a service, they would launch their own. They founded what was originally called L'armement Bretagne-Angleterre-Irlande (BAI) and bought their own freighter, renaming it *Kerisnel* after a small Breton village famous for its cauliflowers.

The facilities were pretty basic on board, with two Portakabin modular buildings lashed to the deck – one with bunk beds for the drivers and the other housing a kitchen to provide meals in transit.

On New Year's Day in 1973, the day of the UK's official entry into the Common Market, 3,000 locals – with French, British and Breton flags flying and a choir singing carols – saw the *Kerisnel* off on its eight-hour journey to Plymouth.

One of the drivers on that original crossing was Tim Deesdale, who 40 years later recalled: "The actual crossing was rough, [however] the crew were very pleasant. It was all very exciting. The food was actually quite good. I honestly believe that sometimes the chef would be dangling string over the side with a hook on it. We had fresh fish – he was catching it!"

That first year Brittany Ferries carried 6,000 lorries, but it had to quickly adapt to an unexpected demand for passenger crossings – Britain's proverbial top 'export'.

In 1974, the *Kerisnel* was replaced by *Penn-Ar-Bed*, which was designed to carry both passengers and vehicles. The success and growing demand for the Plymouth-Roscoff service encouraged the company to order a larger ship, the *Cornouailles*. It entered service in 1977.

New routes were added, and nowadays Brittany Ferries represents a major transport network linking 10 ports in the UK, France, Spain and Ireland. The ships carry nearly 2.5 million passengers, 800,000 cars and 195,000 trucks each year … some of which undoubtedly still carry cauliflowers.

SPARKPOINT: *You must not be afraid to adapt your initial idea when a bigger opportunity emerges.*

Footnote: There is still a strong commitment to providing great food and outstanding service, though the chefs no longer go fishing.

23. HOW TO CREATE THE PERFECT TV SHOW

Predicting a sure-fire hit on TV is said to be almost impossible, which is why it's traditional for networks to commission and test 'pilot' episodes for most of the major shows we now see.

Netflix bucked that trend when in 2012 it commissioned *House of Cards* without a pilot. It was so certain of success that it paid up front for 26 episodes – over 1,200 minutes of TV at a budget of around $100 million.

Netflix believe in the power of data.

They track and analyse a lot of data.

Netflix has over 85 million customers who use their streaming service. It is this large user base that provides all the data they need. Traditional 'broadcast' television networks don't have the same level of access. They get much of their information from surveying samples of people who agree to have their viewing habits recorded.

Another difference is that Netflix has the advantage of being an internet company, meaning they can tap into much more data from all their viewers.

Netflix can track not only what you watch but also:

- When you pause, rewind or fast-forward.
- What day you watch content. (Netflix has found people watch TV shows during the week and movies over the weekend.)
- The date you watch.
- What time you watch content.
- Where you watch.
- What device you use to watch. (Do you like to use your tablet for TV shows? Is children's content watched primarily on iPads?)
- Ratings given via the user review feature (about 4 million per day).
- Searches (about 3 million per day).
- Browsing and scrolling behaviour.

Netflix also looks at data within movies and TV shows. The brand pays people to watch and tag different elements within its programming. Their aim is to provide better recommendations on other films and shows you might like to watch. So rather than the standard genres (Drama, Horror, Sci-Fi), they've created some 80,000 new micro-genres, including 'comedy films featuring talking animals' or 'teen comedy featuring a strong female lead'.

It was the analysis of data like this that led Netflix to conclude that people who loved the original 1990s BBC version of *House of Cards* also liked films starring the actor Kevin Spacey and films directed by David Fincher.

Based on this insight they outbid other networks, including HBO and ABC, for the rights to *House of Cards* and made a new version starring Spacey, with a pilot directed by Fincher.

Jonathan Friedland, former Netflix' Chief Communications Officer, said: "Because we have a direct relationship with consumers, we know what people like to watch and that helps us understand how big the interest is going to be for a given show. It gave us some confidence that we could find an audience for a show like *House of Cards.*"

The rest, as they say, is history. *House of Cards* received high ratings and became a critical success, scooping a host of awards. (Netflix recently came to terms with controversy surrounding Spacey by dropping his character and shifting the focus to actress Robin Wright's character.)

SPARKPOINT: *Insightful analysis of big data can be a source of inspiration for innovation.*

24. A PICTURE IS WORTH A BILLION DOWNLOADS

Relude – which would later become Rovio, the Finnish games-focused entertainment company – was formed by three university friends, Niklas Hed, Jarno Väkeväinen and Kim Dikert.

Together they'd won a mobile game development competition with their multi-player, real-time *King of the Cabbage World*, and they decided to try and turn their passion into a profitable business.

Initially they did well, producing a string of high quality, well performing games that followed the convention of the time: develop a game, launch it, sell what you can and then create another one. Updating an existing game just wasn't done; it was seen as too expensive and unprofitable at the time. The market was product-led, not brand-led.

Things were getting much tougher in the gaming industry as time went by, and it was becoming harder and harder to reach customers in a cost-effective way.

The team had noted the launch of the revolutionary Apple iPhone in 2007 and wondered how they could capitalize on the improved performance and new features of this popular access device. They wanted to create something that was truly 'game-changing', in both senses of the word.

Inspiration would come early in 2009 when a senior game designer, Jaakko Iisalo, presented a single image: a screenshot of a group of angry-looking birds who didn't have wings or even legs. There was only a single picture, but the immediate and extremely positive response led the creative team to believe that they'd found something special.

"In the original concept image, we saw the spark, the mood, the attitude that we needed," said Jaakko. "It was not just pink and fluffy; the emotion was the thing. I had this bunch of birds, and they had this real energy."

The management team were less convinced about a game with birds, but Jaakko and his colleagues didn't give up. "We researched web gaming and discerned what was really popular at that time. We realized that 2D, physics-based games and artillery-based games were very popular. So," he said, "we decided that these would be the areas we would focus on, utilizing the bird characters."

But even from the outset they wanted to 'ruffle the feathers' of the industry and do things differently. "We made a list of parameters to adhere to in creating *Angry Birds*," Jaakko said, "and from the very beginning the idea was to make a big IP (intellectual property). Not just a game, but something much bigger – a brand."

One of those parameters was to create a simple concept, but it wasn't a simple task.

They also recognized the need for distinct characters, and 'Red' was the icon from the start (even if he was originally called George). The yellow-beaked, heavy-browed bird stood out in that first image and he became the first character you would see in the game. Unlike other characters he doesn't have any special powers, but what makes him special is that he's the natural leader. As Jaakko put it, "Red has the smarts to make sure that the team gets through every situation."

The team built a backstory to explain why he gets so angry. Red had found three eggs on Piggy Island and immediately became overly protective. He overreacted to the slightest threat to their safety, 'flying' into a rage.

Angry Birds was launched late in 2009, by which time the business was teetering on the edge of going under … but luckily it immediately took off!

Met with critical acclaim and making great use of the capabilities of the still-emerging iPhone, sales were outstanding.

By May 2012 there had been over a billion downloads of *Angry Birds* across its many platforms, and today it remains the most downloaded app of all time in Apple's App Store.

The brand has since hatched a number of sequels – a successful movie, a series of animated shorts, an array of books – and has collaborated with some of the world's biggest brands, including Lego.

Not bad for an idea based on a single picture.

SPARKPOINT: *Inspiration can be visual as well as verbal or conceptual. As they say, a picture can be worth a thousand words.*

25. AN INNOVATION WORTH DYING FOR?

Elisha Otis truly believed in his innovation, as he was to prove in May 1854 at New York's Crystal Palace, the main exhibition hall of America's first World's Fair.

Standing on top of a hoisting platform, high above the crowds in the grand exhibition hall, he called for everyone's attention. As the heads turned around and up, he swung an axe.

As the sharp blade cut through the rope supporting the platform, the platform began to fall. Shocked silence fell over the hall.

But the platform only dropped a few inches, and then came to a stop.

"All safe, gentlemen!" Elisha announced to the crowd. The inventor's faith in his own revolutionary safety brake had been justified.

Elisha had invented the safety elevator two years earlier, in 1852. He'd solved the problem of suspension rope failure that plagued the elevators of that time with a device of his own design called the Otis Safety Brake (the equivalent of the modern safety gear). In the event of rope failure, a spring would force a ratchet to engage with sawtooth iron bars, stopping and securing the car.

However, he had only sold three up through 1853. Early 1854 was no better, so he decided he would have to do something more radical to promote his invention. And so, he purchased a display at the upcoming Crystal Palace Exhibition.

After his potentially life-threatening show, not only had his faith in his invention been demonstrated but he was to get the commercial rewards he had sought. He sold seven through the remainder of 1854 and another 15 in 1855.

Otis is still the world's leading lift company and it has installed elevators in some of the world's most famous structures, including the Eiffel Tower, Empire State Building, the original World Trade Center, Disney's Twilight Zone Tower of Terror thrill ride, Kuala Lumpur's Petronas Twin Towers, Burj Khalifa in Dubai, Toronto's CN Tower and the Skylon Tower at Niagara Falls.

Many credit his invention as a crucial step in the development of skyscrapers, as it enabled architects and their buildings to reach higher and higher.

All this because Elisha Otis truly believed in his idea … and was willing to put his life on the line to prove it.

SPARKPOINT: *Innovation can call for real commitment.*

26. DOING HER HOMEWORK

By the beginning of the 20th century, coffee drinking was no longer a luxury.

German housewife Melitta Bentz and her husband, Hugo, were among the many people who had recently started to drink it daily, with their breakfast, with cakes and while just sitting and chatting in the afternoon.

However, Melitta's enjoyment was marred by the trials and tribulations of brewing a really good cup. Early percolators were prone to over-brew the coffee, espresso-type machines at the time tended to leave grounds in the drink, and linen filter bags were tiresome to clean.

She was sure that there was a better way. Focusing on the cloth bags that required washing, Melitta started experimenting with different materials. In the end, her homework paid off – or perhaps that should be *her son's* homework paid off!

She noticed a piece of blotting paper her eldest son was using with his fountain pen, which, despite absorbing some of the ink, ultimately let liquid through. Could this be the answer?

Using a nail to poke holes in the bottom of a brass cup, she lined it not with a linen bag but with a sheet of blotting paper from the boy's notebook.

The results were outstanding. Not only did the coffee taste significantly less bitter and more aromatic, but there were no more grounds in the bottom of the cup. And, preparation was fast and simple – there was no bag to wash, as you simply threw away the used 'blotting paper'.

Melitta decided to set up a business, and on 20 June 1908 the Kaiserliche Patentamt (Germany's Imperial Patent Office) granted her a patent. On 15 December 1908 she registered her coffee filter company, 'M. Bentz', with the trade office in Dresden.

Her starting capital was 72 Reichsmark cents, and the company headquarters was a room in her apartment. Her husband Hugo and their sons Horst and Willi became the first employees of the emerging company.

After contracting a tinsmith to manufacture the devices, they sold 1,200 coffee filters at the 1909 Leipzig fair.

In the 1930s, Melitta revised the original filter design, tapering it into the shape of a cone and adding ribs. This created a larger filtration area, allowing for improved extraction of the ground coffee.

In 1936, the widely recognized cone-shaped filter paper that fits inside the tapered filter top was introduced and the brand continued to grow.

Today, more than 80 years later, the company is still in operation and it's still a family affair, run by Melitta's grandchildren.

SPARKPOINT: *Innovation often requires exploration and experimentation.*

27. A STAR IS BORN … ALONG WITH A COW, A DOG AND A QUESTION MARK

Boston Consulting Group is one of the world's leading management consulting firms, serving as an advisor to many businesses, governments and institutions.

The company was founded in 1963 by Bruce Henderson, a Harvard Business School alumnus. Bruce had been recruited by the Boston Safe Deposit and Trust Company (a subsidiary of The Boston Company), where he initially acted as a one-man, one-telephone Management and Consulting Division.

One of BCG's most famous creations is the Boston Matrix, formally known as the Growth-Share Matrix.

This 2x2 matrix was introduced in 1968 and has been used ever since to help companies decide how to allocate investment among their portfolio of business units or products by identifying them as either 'Stars', 'Cash Cows', 'Question Marks' or 'Dogs' (originally 'Pets').

Another of BCG's tenets is the importance of linking the concept of competitive advantage to business strategy, and indeed one of the driving forces of a 'Star' is whether or not it has a clear competitive advantage. As Bruce put it: "Strategy is a deliberate search for a plan of action that will develop a business' competitive advantage and compound it."

Robert Mainer, an early colleague of Bruce's, said that unlike many other consultancies, BCG took their own advice, studying what made them different and what their competitive advantage was.

"He asked what we thought that specialty should be," Robert said. "Many suggestions were offered, but in each case we were able to identify several other firms that already had strong credentials in that particular area. The discussion began to stall."

Then Bruce asked a momentous question: "What about business strategy?"

Robert objected: "That's too vague. Most executives won't know what we're talking about."

"That's the beauty of it," Bruce replied. "We'll define it."

To this day BCG calls itself 'The world's leading advisor on business strategy'.

SPARKPOINT: *Successful innovations should ideally be differentiated from what's already on the market, otherwise why should anyone choose them rather than what already exists?*

28. THE SWEET SMELL OF SUCCESS

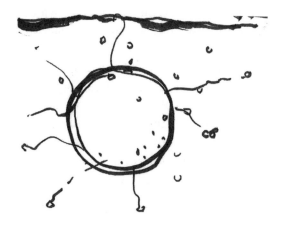

Most brands have values like excellence, integrity, innovative and caring ... but not Lush, the natural cosmetics company famous for its bath ballistics, patented solid shampoo bars and pourable soap.

One of its core values is: 'We believe in the right to make mistakes, lose everything and start again'.

The reason for this fundamental belief started very close to home.

In 1976, Mark and Mo Constantine started formulating and making their own cosmetics in their spare bedroom in the English coastal town of Poole. They went on to establish the hair and beauty products group Constantine & Weir with Elizabeth Weir, now retail director at Lush. They opened a 'Herbal Hair and Beauty Clinic' at 29 High Street in Poole, offering customers treatments with natural, herbal products they'd invented.

One day Mark read about another newly formed company, The Body Shop, and decided to send owner Anita Roddick some samples. These included what he describes as a henna cream shampoo "which looked a bit like you'd just done a poo." She placed an order for £1,200.

The partnership blossomed and Constantine & Weir went on to become The Body Shop's biggest supplier, until in the early '90s Roddick became uncomfortable with the idea that so many of the retailer's product formulations were owned by another company. The Body Shop bought the Constantines out for £6m.*

Mark, Mo and Liz weren't worried, as they had lots more ideas – all those that had been rejected by The Body Shop. They decided to put them all together and, as Mark put it, "pushed them out there in one crazy magazine" – *Cosmetics to Go*.

On one level it was successful, as they started receiving thousands of orders.

There was, however, a problem. "Every time we sent out an order we lost a packet," Mark explained. "We lost money on every transaction and we did millions of transactions."

They hadn't got the business model sorted and were under-pricing. Within two years they had burned through the money they'd been paid for their original business, and they went bust in 1994.

Looking back, the Constantines are very philosophical about the experience. "Actually it was a very healthy thing, as one of the biggest problems businesses have is arrogance, and we are all prone to it, especially people who are confident enough to start their own businesses," said Mark. "So, having a good dose of that taken out of you is probably one of the reasons for Lush's success."

His wife Mo agrees, and now sees that, "It was the learning that helped shape the basic principles for Lush."

They decided to start again, back in their original store in Poole.

While they were much more focused on the money side of the business this time around, that didn't stop them from creating one of the most distinctive and sensory-rich shopping experiences on the High Street.

The look of a Lush shop was partly inspired by the London Cheese Shop in Neal's Yard. Lush's soaps are sold in wedges that look like cheese. They're priced by weight and then wrapped in greaseproof paper. 'Bath bombs' are piled up like fruit, and the 'butter cream' looks more like a mouth-watering cake than shower soap.

The amazing fragrances you smell as you approach any of their stores comes from the brand policy of avoiding packaging wherever possible. It acts not only as a sensory advertisement, but as Mark jokes it is, "The sweet smell of success."

The company's new name, Lush, came courtesy of one of their old customers, all of whom had been asked for suggestions.

By 1995, the first Lush was doing well enough to allow the team to open a second and third shop in Covent Garden and King's Road. The locations paid off as celebrities like Madonna and Julia Roberts were seen buying their soap and bath bombs and the PR skyrocketed awareness of the new brand.

Lush has now grown from that single store in Poole, Dorset, to a 400+ strong chain, including 80 locations in Britain and others in North America, Japan and Australia.

> **SPARKPOINT:** *Creating a rich sensory experience can add value to your innovation.*

29. AFTER THE BURN, BOOM

Will King had a problem – a nasty, recurring problem. Every day after shaving he would suffer from razor burn. His neck would be red and sore all morning.

He tried different foams and gels with no success; still he got the razor burn.

One day he noticed a bottle of his girlfriend's baby oil sitting next to his shaving foam. She used it as a moisturizer for soothing and smoothing her skin. He got to wondering what would happen if he mixed them together.

Curious to see what would happen, he mixed up a batch and tried it.

"Although the razor got gummed up and the bathroom sink got rather messy, I didn't get the dreaded burn,"

Will said. "I'd had what would turn out to be the first of many *King of Shaves*."

Will's next step was to improve the formulation. His objective was to retain all the smoothness he wanted but reduce the tendency of the mix to gum the blades up. Cue a messy kitchen table as Will experimented with mixing different oils.

Finally, having created what he believed was a winning formula, he found a supplier, and using his limited capital produced an initial run of 9,600 bottles of his new 'King of Shaves' gel.

His skill as a salesman was the next challenge, but as he said, "I managed to get it listed in Harrods, and then a year later Boots stocked it. Boom! I was off."

King of Shaves is now the third-largest shaving brand in the UK, and in addition to the gels it sells its own razors as well.

For his part, Will is now clean-shaven, razor-burn free and the owner of a highly successful brand.

SPARKPOINT: *Despite the desire for more and more research, sometimes a sample of one is enough.*

30. THE QUEENS WHO STOLE BARBIE'S CROWN

Taofick Okoya was shocked and saddened when his daughter told him that she wished she were white.

On reflection, he realized that perhaps this wasn't so surprising. In Nigeria, as in many other countries, there is a huge amount of Western influence and it has an impact on all aspects of daily life. Furthermore, Taofick noticed that this socio-cultural influence wasn't just affecting his daughter but seemed to be increasingly pervasive among her friends and children across the country.

It was an insight that would change his future.

Having understood that this influence started to affect people from an early age, he decided he would launch a brand that would take on one of the West's most famous children's cultural icons. He created dolls that took on the might of the toymaker Mattel and challenged Barbie's role as 'queen' of young girls' hearts.

Interviewed in *Elle* magazine, Taofick explained his thinking: "I don't believe Mattel sees the Nigerian market as a priority, yet their product has great influence on the psyche of the children here and affirms certain values contrary to our society."

He reasoned that this Western influence was likely responsible for his daughter wishing she were white. "It made me aware that I needed to make her proud and happy being a black African girl, and not limit it to her alone, as this was a common trend among the younger generation," he said. "The Queens of Africa became a platform to achieve this."

So, in 2007, Taofick launched his Queens of Africa range of dolls, which he felt Nigerian girls would better identify with, since they reflected their skin colour and clothing styles. The dolls, which cost around £4.50, were modelled on three of the country's biggest tribes and come with traditional outfits and accessories. Their aim is to promote strong feminine ideals, like love, peace and endurance.

According to Reuters, the dolls are now selling up to 9,000 units a month – accounting for a staggering 15% of the country's toy market – and are so successful that they're outselling Barbie in Nigeria. The Queens of Africa programme now includes dolls, books, comics, music and an animation series.

Thanks to a strong online presence, customers are also coming from as far afield as Europe, Brazil and America.

Taofick's daughter wasn't interviewed, but I expect she's now pretty proud of her dad and her heritage.

SPARKPOINT: *Though not always easy to achieve, a desire to change the world can be a powerful source of inspiration.*

31. DO ONE THING AND DO IT PROPERLY

You can retell a story or sometimes you can just let the 'hero' tell their own story. This is how Tom Byng tells the story of the beginnings of the Byron restaurant chain.

"The Byron story hails from the misspent nights of my youth," is how Tom tells it.

"During a four-year stint in America, I ate enough hamburgers to sink the Titanic," he said. "My favourite diner was the Silver Top in downtown Providence, Rhode Island. I would end up there, late at night, frequently a little worse for wear, with two or three friends. We always ordered hamburgers. They were simple, tasty things – a bit messy, but made with good quality meat and only the classic adornments: some lettuce, tomato, red onion and maybe a slice of cheese or bacon. The ultimate comfort food, and so satisfying in their simplicity."

They were, as he saw it, hamburgers the way they should be.

Living back in London in 2007, it struck him that there weren't any restaurants offering hamburgers like those at the Silver Top. "So," he said, "the idea for Byron was born: to do a simple thing, and do it well and do it properly.

"We source good beef from Scotland. We mince it fresh every day. We cook it medium so it's pink, juicy and succulent. We place it in a soft, squishy bun with minimum fuss and fanfare. We serve it with a smile in a comfortable environment. And that's it," he said.

"We have a few restaurants now but our vision remains the same: to keep serving proper hamburgers the way they should be."

SPARKPOINT: *Can you be the first to bring something new to a market, and can you 'steal with pride'?*

32. THE PRISONER AND THE BROOM

They say that inspiration can strike at any time or in any place, but a spell in London's Newgate Prison in 1780 wouldn't be my first guess on the origins of an innovation that we all still use, not once but twice a day.

William Addis was born in 1734. He became a stationer, collecting and then pulping old rags before turning them into high quality paper. He would then sell this paper to printers and booksellers across London.

It is worth noting that 18th century booksellers would also often sell patent medicines and supplies for pharmacies. This may have been one factor in sparking William's creativity, but it was definitely something that would later help him gain distribution for his idea.

William appears to have been a colourful character, and one night in 1780 he was picked up in Spitalfields, charged with causing a riot and thrown into Newgate Prison.

Not surprisingly, while serving his time he got bored. One day he noticed a broom in the corner, and the germ of an idea sprang to mind.

Not everyone in those days cleaned their teeth, and those who did either chewed sticks or rubbed their teeth with a rag and a combination of salt and soot. William wondered if he had found a better way to do things.

He found a small animal bone and made some holes in it. He managed to scrounge some bristles off one of his guards and threaded these through the holes, fixing them with glue. All told, it had been a short jump from a floor broom to the modern toothbrush.

Once he was at liberty again, William founded a new company in Whitechapel and started making brushes from animal bone and horsehair under the Addis brand name.

Initial distribution was through his old contacts in the book trade. What's more, William's timing was good. Refined sugar was a relatively new but increasingly popular foodstuff for Georgian era Londoners, and anything that might help prevent rotten teeth was highly desirable.

Sales grew quickly.

William experimented with different types of bristles, including badger hair, but the most efficacious was found to be hair from the Siberian boar. It wouldn't be until the 1940s that a toothbrush with nylon tufts would be introduced, under the Wisdom brand name.

SPARKPOINT: *Inspiration can be found anywhere –*
never stop looking.

Footnote: For those who know my work, the title of this story of course
plays off the title of my first book of stories, *The Prisoner and the Penguin*.

33. GET ON YOUR BIKE AND INNOVATE

Innovation isn't just about new products or services; sometimes it's about doing the same thing but doing it better.

In 2010, Dave Brailsford became the new General Manager and Performance Director for Team Sky, Great Britain's professional cycling team. He was given the unenviable task of ensuring that a British cyclist won the Tour de France, something that had never happened in the 100+ years the race had been run.

Dave believed that if all went to plan, Team Sky could be in a position to win the Tour de France within five years. Just three years later, they actually won it.

How did he and his team achieve this? Was there a single thing that made the difference?

The answer, of course, is that it wasn't one single thing that made all the difference, but rather a whole series of them.

Dave believed in the notion of *multiplicity in action*. He set out not to change one thing but to look for improvements in everything, an approach that he called the 'aggregation of marginal gains'. He and his team would search for what he described as, "the 1% margin for improvement in everything you do."

His belief was that if you improved every area related to cycling by just 1%, then those small gains would add up to remarkable improvement.

They started on what were perhaps the more obvious aspects of performance: the riders' nutrition, their weekly training programme, the ergonomics of the bike seat and the weight of the tyres.

This was, however, just the beginning. Dave and his team went in search of those 1% improvements in even the smallest areas, which weren't so obvious and were overlooked by most other teams. They found the pillow that helped the riders get the best night's sleep and took it with them to hotels. They tested numerous massage gels before choosing the one that was most effective. They even taught their riders the best way to wash their hands to avoid infection.

Then, in 2012, with these and countless other small improvements under their belts, Team Sky rider Sir Bradley Wiggins became the first British cyclist to win the Tour de France.

SPARKPOINT: *Innovation isn't just about new products or services, sometimes it's about doing the same thing but better.*

34. FROM CONVENT GIRL TO MISTRESS TO THE SWEET SMELL OF SUCCESS

She was the daughter of a market-stall holder and a laundry woman in Saumur, in France's Loire Valley, but after her mother died she was sent to a Cistercian convent where she would spend her teenage years.

By1909 things had changed, just a bit, and she arrived in Paris as the mistress of the textile baron Étienne Balsan.

She set up a millinery boutique under Étienne's apartment, and by 1920 she had become a phenomenon in French fashion circles. She ran a series of successful boutiques in Paris, Deauville and Biarritz.

She owned a villa in the south of France and drove around in a blue Rolls Royce. She was the belle of the

Parisian elite and had a retinue of friends and admirers among the city's 'racy' women. But she still wanted more.

She was fastidiously clean, and when working with many of her clients she would complain about the way they smelled, stinking of musk and body odour.

She decided to create a scent that could describe the new, modern woman she epitomized – 'a woman's perfume, with a woman's scent' – and once Coco Chanel had decided something she went about achieving it.

During the late summer of 1920, Coco went on holiday to the Côte d'Azur with her current lover, the Grand Duke Dmitri Pavlovich. There she learned of a perfumer, a sophisticated and well-read character named Ernest Beaux, who had worked for the Russian royal family and lived close by in Grasse, the centre of the perfume industry.

Ernest took up Coco's challenge and after several months he presented her with ten samples he'd formulated. They were numbered one to five and 20 to 24.

One of the samples, whether by mistake or design (a question that's still the matter of some debate), contained a larger than normal dose of aldehyde.

This was unusual because in those days the normal way to create fresh fragrances was to use citrus such as lemon, bergamot and orange, but none of these lasted on the skin. Chemists had isolated chemicals called aldehydes that could artificially create these smells, but because they were very powerful perfumers were hesitant to use them.

Coco chose the sample with the abundant aldehyde. "It was what I was waiting for," she later said. "A perfume like nothing else."

It was a formulation that probably subconsciously appealed to her desire for cleanness and freshness.

And the number of the sample – No. 5 of course.

To celebrate, she invited Ernest and other friends to a popular upmarket restaurant on the Riviera and sprayed the perfume around the table. It is said that every woman who passed by stopped and asked what the fragrance was and where it came from.

Coco was now certain she had another success on her hands, or rather her neck.

And while the brand is now famous for its celebrity endorsements, from the likes of Marilyn Monroe, Catherine Deneuve, Suzy Parker, Candice Bergen, Lauren Hutton, Nicole Kidman, Audrey Tatou and Gisele Bündchen; one of the first models used in the advertising was Coco herself.

SPARKPOINT: *If at times you can't do it yourself, don't be afraid to work with relevant experts – but make sure you stay true to what you want.*

35. LAUNCHING A BRAND MAY NOT BE CHILD'S PLAY BUT IT CAN BE A CHILDREN'S BOOK

By now, dear reader, you will have gathered that I love the stories behind brands, and I like to retell them, but even I don't often come across the story of the birth of a brand that is the subject of a children's storybook and features a court case.

Southwest Airlines is no ordinary brand. It is renowned for its culture, its sense of humour and as a pioneer of low-cost flying.

The 'boring' story of the brand actually begins in a restaurant where two friends, Rollin King and Herb Kelleher, meet for dinner. During the meal Rollin drew a triangle on a paper napkin, a simple visual of his concept for an airline that would connect Dallas, Houston and San Antonio.

The pair incorporated their idea as Air Southwest on 15 March 1967, but it would be four years before the brand would 'take-off'.

At the time, there were a number of established airlines flying in and out of the same Texas cities. They included Braniff, Aloha Airlines, United Airlines, Trans-Texas and Continental Airlines. These airlines initiated legal action, alleging that Air Southwest was violating US cost controls and market regulations, and thus began a three-year court battle to keep the fledgling airline firmly grounded.

Air Southwest eventually prevailed in the Texas Supreme Court and won the right to fly in that state. The decision became final on 7 December 1970, when the United States Supreme Court declined to review the case.

A few years later, in 1981, a children's book writer and illustrator named Winifred Barnum-Newman was taking a flight on what was now called Southwest Airlines. She was struck by how 'cute' the plane looked, and once the flight had taken off she took out her sketchbook and started drawing it.

When Winifred returned home those sketches got filed away with other ideas, but two months later she found them again and decided to give the head of marketing at Southwest Airlines a call. He immediately recognized her name, as his daughter had one of Winifred's other books. When he heard what she had done he asked if he could see the sketches, and after she'd sent them to him the executive asked Winifred to fly up and meet him.

After some discussions, Winifred – who by now had read the story of the fight for the right to fly – said she wanted to do a book that would appeal to both children and their parents. She pitched it as being all about the court case.

Winifred recalls the marketing exec's initial reaction: "Ooooh-kay ... you want to do a book about a court case for children."

Two weeks later, however, when Winifred presented the first draft of the manuscript and some initial sketches, he was bowled over.

They decided to send it to the airline's CEO, Herb Kelleher, to see what he thought. Again, the initial response was quick but much more positive. He sent back a short note: "I love it."

The book *Gumwrappers and Goggles* was published in 1983. Carefully avoiding further court cases, it tells the story of TJ Love, a small jet who's taken to court by two larger jets to keep him from their hangar, and then to try and stop him from flying at all. Justice is served when TJ Love's right to fly is upheld after an impassioned plea from his lawyer.

No company names are mentioned in the book, but TJ Love's colours just happen to be those of Southwest Airlines, and the two other jets are coloured in Braniff's and Continental's colours.

The lawyer who gives the decisive speech bears more than a passing resemblance to Herb, Southwest's chief executive.

The book was later adapted into a stage musical, *Show Your Spirit*, sponsored by Southwest Airlines, and ran in towns served by the airline.

SPARKPOINT: *Coming up with an idea isn't the only problem; you may need to fight off competition.*

36. WHY QUALITY IS NOT ENOUGH

Many people believe that a high quality product is all you need to build a successful brand, but in fact quality is only part of the story.

William Hough Watson was a Bolton chemist who in the 1880s created a new type of soap using glycerine and vegetable oils, such as palm oil, rather than the traditional tallow (animal fats).

However, the real success of the brand was actually down to William Lever and his brother James Darcy Lever.

They observed that consumers had no guarantee of consistent quality, given the way soap was produced and sold at the time.

Soap was sold through grocery stores that were more like frontier trading posts. If you wanted some soap, you asked the grocer to cut you a piece off a large block he kept behind the counter. Not only would that soap be of unknown origin and uncertain quality, if it was good you had no guarantee of getting the same thing the next time you came back.

The Lever brothers overcame this problem by deciding to package small blocks of soap and give the product an appropriate name. And so, Sunlight became the world's first packaged, branded laundry soap when it was introduced in 1884.

The brand and its promise of consistent quality helped ensure its lasting success, and in 1888 it lent its name to the village that was built to house Lever's factory workers: Port Sunlight.

SPARKPOINT: *If your idea is just about quality it may not be enough – you may need something more to offer your customers.*

37. FROM BEADS TO BOARDS TO BECOMING A BILLIONAIRE

Nick Woodman was a failure, or at least his first two entrepreneurial attempts were.

His first start-up was an e-commerce brand – EmpowerAll.com – that aimed to sell electronics products for a mere 2% mark-up. Unfortunately, it tanked … and fast.

Nick's second endeavour, for which he managed to raise $3.9 million, was Funbug, 'a gaming and marketing platform that gives users the chance to win cash prizes'.

Like so many tech start-ups of the early 2000s, it didn't gain traction and quickly burnt through its money.

He needed a break, and a chance to lick his wounds, so like any good Californian Nick decided to go surfing.

It proved to be the right thing to do in more ways than he expected. While recharging his batteries he would identify a problem, and in solving it he'd create the basis for a multi-million dollar brand.

The problem Nick encountered was close to his heart and his love of surfing. It was how to capture the thrill and excitement of riding a 'barrel' – the curling cylinder of space inside a wave. Surfing is usually filmed from afar, often from the shore or maybe off a boat or jet ski. Nick wanted to capture images from the inside-out, not outside-in.

His solution was to attach a camera to his wrist. His first prototype was made out of a broken surfboard leash and rubber bands, which allowed him to dangle a Kodak disposable camera from his wrist for easy operation when he caught the perfect wave.

Brad Schmidt, a friend who would later become GoPro's creative director, met Nick in Indonesia and made some suggested improvements, including the need for a more durable camera, one that could take the wear and tear of the sea.

Returning to California, Nick felt he was really onto something this time.

He borrowed $200,000 from his father, and from his mother $35,000 and a sewing machine, which he would use to sew the different camera straps he tried while experimenting with early designs. He and his future wife, Jill, generated an additional $10,000 by selling shell necklaces they bought in Bali.

He eventually put together something he was happy with and took his first product to market – a combination of a 35mm film camera developed by Hotax, his custom wrist strap and camera housing, and the new GoPro name and logo.

This time around Nick and his new brand were to prove successful.

He made his first big sale in 2004 when a Japanese company ordered 100 cameras at a sports show. The following year Nick appeared on the QVC home-shopping network to sell his GoPro Hero.

Sales soared and by 2012 GoPro was selling over 2 million cameras a year. Along the way, the products have evolved and they now include compact digital cameras that support Wi-Fi, can be remotely controlled, have better waterproof housing and record to a micro SD card.

In December 2012 the Taiwanese contract manufacturer Foxconn purchased 8.88% of the company for $200 million, which set its market value at $2.25 billion and made Nick, who owned the majority of the stock, a billionaire.

GoPro went public on June 26 2014, closing the day at $31.34 a share.

In 2014, Nick was the highest paid US chief executive, paying himself $235 million while GoPro earned annual profits of $128 million.

Not bad for a 'failure'.

SPARKPOINT: *Early prototyping allows you to develop ideas faster.*

38. FROM BIOMIMICRY TO METONYMY VIA PORTMANTEAU

George de Mestral, a Swiss engineer, used to take his dog with him when he went out hunting in the Alps. After these days out, in the early 1940s, he would often have to spend time pulling off the burrs that clung to his trousers and his dog's fur.

He was curious about how and why this happened, so he took one of the burdock burrs and looked at it under a microscope. He could now see the hundreds of tiny 'hooks' that caught onto anything with a loop, such as clothing, animal fur or hair, and started to wonder if he could somehow turn this natural phenomena into something useful.

Luckily George was a patient man, because it took him nearly eight years of trying before he could successfully reproduce a form of this natural attachment system. He used two strips of fabric, one with thousands of tiny hooks and another with thousands of tiny loops. It was to become one of the most famous examples of what is called biomimicry – an invention inspired by nature.

Over the long period of experimentation, he had plenty of time to think about how such an invention could be used and identified its potential to fasten things together, in a way that could then be easily undone. It was an idea that would be described as 'The zipper-less zipper'.

In deciding on a name for his new product, like the product itself George chose something that had two separate elements which when combined created something new. He chose a portmanteau word, comprising the words 'velvet' and 'crochet', and christened it *Velcro*.

He formally patented his invention in 1955.

The first Velcro was made out of cotton, but George soon discovered that nylon worked better because it didn't wear out with continued use.

Sales of Velcro took off, or rather *blasted off* when in the early 1960s the Apollo astronauts started using it to secure pens, food packets and equipment they didn't want floating away in the weightlessness of space.

The resulting PR encouraged all sorts of other applications. Hospitals used it on the straps of blood pressure gauges and on patient gowns. It was used in trains, planes and automobiles as fasteners for floor mats, slipcovers and seat cushions. And in 1968, Puma became the first major shoe company to offer a sneaker with Velcro fasteners.

In 1984, David Letterman interviewed Velcro's US director of industrial sales while wearing a Velcro suit. When the interview was over, he launched himself via trampoline onto a Velcro wall. Another new use for Velcro was created – outfits for 'human fly' contests.

By the late 1980s Velcro's original patent had expired and companies in Europe, Mexico and Asia started making their own versions of the product. Although there is only one brand that is legally allowed to call itself Velcro, many of the imitators' products are generically referred to as Velcro.

Velcro had joined that select band of metonymy brands whose names are, in common parlance, used to refer to an entire category of product. Others include Ziploc, Kleenex, Sellotape and Guinness.

So now you know how Velcro began, and may have had your vocabulary enriched in the process!

SPARKPOINT: *Biomimicry is a natural source of inspiration.*

39. HEADLINE NEWS – HOW TO BEAT THE FLU

Dr Franklin Miles established Dr Miles' Medical Company in 1884, in Elkhart, Indiana. (It changed its name to Miles Laboratories in 1935.)

By 1890, the sales success of his patent medicine tonic – *Dr Miles' Nervine*, which claimed to treat 'nervousness or nervous exhaustion, sleeplessness, hysteria, headache, neuralgia, backache, pain, epilepsy, spasms, fits, and St Vitus's dance' – allowed him to develop a mail order medicine business.

To fill the mail order catalogue the company was always on the lookout for new 'medicines' that it could market. So, during a severe flu epidemic in 1928, Hub Beardsley, then president of Miles Lab, visited the local newspaper where it was rumoured that all the employees remained fit and healthy.

Talking to Tom Keene, the editor, Hub discovered their secret – all the employees took a mix of aspirin and baking soda at the first sign of illness and, quite miraculously, did not succumb to the dreaded flu.

Hub decided that this might be an opportunity and asked his chief chemist, Maurice Treneer, to come up with a similar concoction that the company could market. The chemist got to work and made up some samples.

Hub then took 100 of these tablets with him on a cruise, and as people exhibited early symptoms of the flu he passed out his free samples. He was pleasantly surprised to find that they actually worked.

The product, Alka-Seltzer, was launched on 21 February 1931.

Still, the old habit of claiming that their medicines were efficacious in many ways lead to early advertisements claiming that the new brand was suitable for 'colds, headaches, gas on the stomach, sour stomach, simple neuralgia, muscular aches and pains, that tired feeling, that morning-after feeling, rheumatic fever and muscular lumbago'.

SPARKPOINT: *Keep your ears and your eyes open; you never know what you'll find.*

40. **TOO SWEET?**

When your younger brother decides to go into the family business and transforms it into what will eventually become General Motors of Canada, you might feel it would be difficult to top that.

However, John James 'Jack' McLaughlin is probably as famous as his younger brother, automotive pioneer and philanthropist Robert Samuel McLaughlin, because it was Jack who invented 'the champagne of ginger ales'.

Jack studied pharmacy at Ontario College in Toronto but moved to Brooklyn to complete his qualifications. While studying he earned some money at a drug store where he operated the soda fountain, mixing fruit-flavoured syrups with carbonated water and ice. The drinks were extravagantly named, with monikers like Humdinger, American Gentleman, Happy Hooligan, Gunther's Excelsior, Pugilists' Panacea and Japanese Thirst Killer.

Seeing how successful soda was becoming in New York, when Jack moved back to Canada in the early 1890s he decided to set up a drinks store near Old City Hall in Toronto.

He wasn't the only person to have spotted the opportunity – at least a dozen rival soda companies were established around the same time. However, Jack did well and soon moved to larger premises on Berti Street near Queen and Church, where he employed his first staff: two men and a driver.

It was here that Jack began mixing flavoured fruit syrups with sparkling water to make 'pop'. An early success was Tona-Cola, nicknamed 'Ton O' Coal', a play on the way the name was pronounced. Like other sodas, it was sold through druggists, grocers and from soda fountains at five cents a glass.

Another early product was a spicy 'McLaughlin's Belfast Style Ginger Ale', similar to an old-style ginger beer. However, a number of customers complained that it was too dark and syrupy. Jack saw an opportunity to offer something lighter and more refined, and in 1904 created a new product described in early adverts as having 'a snap and a tingle; a smart spry taste'.

Jack named it after his homeland and for its different taste profile – Canada Dry Pale Ginger Ale – and the original logo combined an image of a beaver with a map of Canada. It was Jack's wife, Maud, who came up with what would become the best-known slogan for the brand: The champagne of ginger ales.

It was a great success and Jack opened plants in Edmonton and Winnipeg to help with national distribution. The trade name was registered to the company in 1907.

The drink was even appointed to The Royal Household of the Governor General of Canada, and to reflect this the beaver was removed from the logo in favour of a crown, and the map of Canada was placed inside a shield, as it appears on the label today.

Its popularity as a mixer grew further during Prohibition, when its flavour helped mask the poor taste of many of the era's rough, homemade liquors.

Today the brand is owned by the Dr Pepper Snapple Group, Inc., and is one of Canada's most famous home-grown brands.

I'm sure Jack would drink to that.

SPARKPOINT: *A premium version of an existing product can often be an opportunity.*

41. **2M**

The idea of Mars and Hershey collaborating on new product development might seem far-fetched today, but shortly after World War II the two companies came together to create one of the world's largest confectionary brands.

Forrest Mars Sr was the son of Frank C Mars, the founder of the Mars Company, but after his parents' divorce he was raised in Canada by his mother and rarely saw his father. After high school he entered the University of California at Berkeley and later transferred to Yale University.

After finishing his degree in industrial engineering, Forrest joined his father at Mars, Inc., but the collaboration didn't last long. Father and son disagreed over whether to expand abroad. Forrest wanted to, while his father did not.

Forrest moved to Europe, where he worked briefly for Nestlé and the Tobler Company before inventing the Mars bar while in England in 1933. This was to prove to be a successful addition to Mars' growing range of confectionery products.

He also travelled to Spain, where during the Spanish Civil War he saw soldiers eating chocolate pellets covered with a hard shell of tempered chocolate that prevented the centre from melting. That sowed the seed for an idea that was to come to fruition some years later.

Forrest returned to the US and started his own food business, Food Products Manufacturing, creating the Uncle Ben's Rice line and a gourmet food business, Pedigree.

However, an idea he'd had in Spain had been slowly germinating, and shortly before World War II Forrest struck a deal to develop the idea with Bruce Murrie, who was also the son of a famous businessman. Bruce's father was none other than William F R Murrie, the long-time president of Hershey's.

Forrest received a patent for the production process for a new type of candy on 3 March 1941, and production began later that year in New Jersey. They decided to call the hard-sugar-coated chocolate they'd created M&M's, which stood for Mars and Murrie. They were promoted as the chocolate that 'melts in your mouth, not in your hands'.

This deal with Bruce was to prove particularly valuable during the war period, helping ensure that the new brand continued to get a supply of chocolate, since Hershey had control of all of America's rationed chocolate at the time.

In 1948 Forrest bought out Bruce's interest, and Mars and Hersey went from being 'partners' to fierce competitors.

And the moral of the story is that there is sometimes a thin line between partner and competitor. How could partnering with a competitor benefit you both?

SPARKPOINT: *Travel is a great source of inspiration.*

42. LE MARKETING EST ARRIVÉ: HOW BEAUJOLAIS NOUVEAU RACED TO THE TOP

When you think about races in France, the first two that probably come to mind are 'Le Tour de France' and 'Le Mans', but it is a third race that has seen by far the greatest variety of 'vehicles'.

Contestants have used cars, trucks, motorcycles, balloons, helicopters, rickshaws, elephants and even a Concorde jet to compete in it.

It's a race that, for the last 50 years or so, has started at one minute past midnight on the third Thursday of November. It runs from a region just north of Lyon to the capital, Paris, and the contestants all carry the same thing – that year's Beaujolais Nouveau wine.

While Beaujolais Nouveau has a much longer history, it is only in these last 50 years that the annual release of that year's vintage has become a globally known and celebrated event.

The region of France known as Beaujolais is 34 miles long and varies from seven to nine miles wide. It is home to nearly 4,000 vineyards that produce the 12 officially designated types of Beaujolais known as AOCs (Appellation d'Origine Controlee). These include some of the finest and priciest grand cru wines, including Fleurie and Côte de Brouilly. The most common two are the Beaujolais and Beaujolais-Villages, but it is Beaujolais Nouveau that is the most famous.

Beaujolais Nouveau started life as the region's 'vin de l'année' (annual wine), bottled to celebrate the end of the harvest. Drunk in the local bars, cafés and bistros of Beaujolais and nearby Lyons, it was made very quickly and intended to be consumed immediately – taking only weeks from grape to glass. The other Beaujolais wines take a much more leisurely course.

In 1937 the Beaujolais AOC was established to help protect and promote the quality of wines produced in the region, but the initial AOC rules meant that Beaujolais wine could only be officially sold after 15 December in the year of harvest.

It wasn't until after World War II, in 1951, that this rule was relaxed and the date was brought forward to 15 November. One consequence was that the vin de l'année became known as Beaujolais Nouveau. Despite these changes, sales of the Nouveau stayed modest and mostly local.

A few years later, three men came up with a novel plan to try and promote the occasion and the wine. Jean Tixier, an executive at Havas advertising agency, Georges Duboeuf, who founded and ran a wine 'house' (brand), and Pierre Boisset, a broker at the wine merchant Nicolas, came up with the idea of making a marketing event out of the release day. The Beaujolais Nouveau race and the slogan 'Le Beaujolais Nouveau est arrivé' were born.

The race – which centred on being the first to deliver the new harvest's wine to Paris – quickly became a phenomenon, first in France, then across Europe, and by the 1970s it was starting to generate worldwide publicity. In the 1980s and '90s the race itself was expanded to include new final destinations in Japan and the US.

In 1985 the date was again changed, to the third Thursday of November, another clever marketing move to ensure that it was always available just before a weekend and to be close to Thanksgiving in the US, which was by then and remains a major market.

The long-running slogan was changed in 2005 to 'It's Beaujolais Nouveau time'.

Nowadays over 70 million bottles, nearly half of the region's total annual production, will be Beaujolais Nouveau.

Georges Duboeuf remains a tireless promoter and more than a fifth of his annual production, about 4 million bottles, is Beaujolais Nouveau.

SPARKPOINT: *Though most of the stories in this book are about new products and services, innovation can relate to new forms of communication and activation too.*

43. IN THE BEGINNING WAS THE WORD, NOW THERE IS THE APP

The digital age has brought many benefits, but for Bobby Gruenewald it has been a 'godsend' in his mission to get people to become more engaged with the Bible.

Bobby is the CEO of YouVersion, a Bible app, which has been downloaded to over 100 million devices and is opened by some 66,000 people every second of the day or night. Bobby says he knows of one woman who "would stay up until just past midnight to know what verse she had received for her next day."

In an interview with author Nir Eyal, Bobby explained how they use digital best practices to help ensure regular engagement of YouVersion's 'flock'. "We originally started as a desktop website, but that really didn't engage people in the Bible," he said. "It wasn't until we tried a mobile version that we noticed a difference in people, including ourselves, turning to the Bible more because it was on a device they always had on them."

Users can now turn to the scripture wherever they are; Bobby's data even suggests that 18% of readers have used it in the bathroom.

Other features designed to encourage regular engagement include 400 themed reading plans. "By offering reading plans with different small sections of the Bible each day, it helps keep (readers) from giving up," he said. Bite-size chunks of what is a long book makes usage easier, but so too does the order in which they're presented. Positioning sections that are more interesting early in the plan helps create the daily habit, before some of the more difficult or boring sections are sent.

While initially concerned about pestering readers with notifications, an experiment helped convince YouVersion of its potential. "For Christmas, we sent people a message from the app," Bobby explained. "Just a 'Merry Christmas' in various languages. We were afraid people would uninstall the app, but just the opposite happened. People took pictures of the notification on their phones and started sharing them on Instagram, Twitter and Facebook. They felt God was reaching out to them."

Nowadays a wide variety of these notifications are used to trigger usage. There is a daily notification sent to your phone. If that doesn't work there is a little red light that activates above the YouVersion Bible icon on your device. If you miss your first day of a plan, a message is sent suggesting an alternative plan.

To make usage even easier there's also an option whereby you can have the extract read to you.

The power of peer encouragement is built in too. Members can and do send messages to each other and, of course, there is much sharing on social media sites.

Perhaps not surprisingly there is a regular usage spike on Sundays, which YouVersion further encourages through a service where religious leaders can upload their sermons into the app. The congregation can then follow along in real time in church.

Bobby has many stories about the good the app has done, but one of his favourites is undoubtedly the one that was told to him by a user who had walked into a business you might not associate with devout Christians. The man's phone beeped as a YouVersion notification arrived. Gruenewald recalls the user telling him his thoughts: "God's trying to tell me something! I just walked into a strip club – and, man – the Bible just texted me!" The user turned and walked right out.

SPARKPOINT: *Think about how new channels and technology can help you engage with your audience better.*

44. THE EYES HAVE IT

The origins of some brands have been lost, while for other brands they are blessed with a number of alternative stories of their beginnings.

One of these brands is Maybelline, which has two stories.

Both stories have similarities, including the presence of Tom Lyle Williams, sometimes referred to as TL, and his sister Mabel Williams.

The first and by far the most romantic version, however, introduces us to Chet, the object of Mabel's affections.

It holds that in 1915 Mabel was getting worried. She had started hearing whispers that her boyfriend, Chet Hewes, was falling for another woman. She confided in T L, and being a loving brother he decided he must do something about it.

Now T L was a chemist, and he was interested in cosmetics. He mixed coal dust and Vaseline, and told Mabel to apply the resulting concoction to her eyelashes to improve their colour and overall look.

As this love story goes, Mabel then not only won Chet back, but the couple were married a year later. They went on to have three children and lived happily together for nearly 50 wonderful years.

The brand story goes on to tell how T L developed the product commercially, christening it 'Maybelline' – a combination of the words Mabel and Vaseline.

Unfortunately for all you romantics, it seems that this is the less likely of the two stories, as the other is drawn from a number of sources, including *The Maybelline Story* by Sharrie Williams, a direct descendant of the Williams siblings.

However, the beginning of her story is still the source of some family debate, as she explained in a recent blog.

"I grew up hearing the story from my grandmother and father," she wrote. "They said she (Mabel) had very pale brows and lashes and wanted to darken them, so concocted a mixture of ash and Vaseline to make them appear darker. Another story came from Mabel's sister Eva, who said she accidentally singed her lashes and brows while cooking over the stove. Yet another story floated around the family saying Mabel had some kind of disease that made her brows and lashes fall out. I chose the singed brows and lashes version for my book, *The Maybelline Story*, only to be corrected after the book came out by Mabel's two daughters, Shirley and Joyce. They say their mother accidentally bleached her brows."

Whichever of these it was, the year was still 1915, and it was Mabel who first mixed petroleum jelly with coal dust and ash from a burnt cork, and applied it to her lashes and brows. T L sat nearby, fascinated as Mabel performed what she called 'a secret of the harem' (or alternatively a trick she got from *Photoplay* magazine).

Seeing an opportunity for a product to sell through his fledgling mail order business, T L used a home chemistry set to produce a mixture containing petrolatum (Vaseline), carbon black, cottonseed oil and safflower oil. Unfortunately, when his consumer test sample – Mabel – applied it to her lashes, it ran into her eyes and stung them badly.

Undaunted, T L sought professional advice and commissioned Parke-Davis, a wholesale drug manufacturer, to develop a more suitable product. The result was a scented cream consisting of refined white petrolatum along with several oils to add sheen. It did not contain any colouring agent but it seemed to 'brighten the eyes'. He called the product 'Lash-Brow-Ine'. The term mascara would not be introduced until 1933.

An advertisement for Lash-Brow-Ine ran in *Photoplay* in 1916. As cash came in, it was used to place adverts in other magazines, such as *Pictorial Review, The Deliniator* and *The Saturday Evening Post*, and so the business grew.

T L invested some of this increased revenue in new product development, and in 1917 – again with the assistance of Parke-Davis – 'Maybell Laboratories' began production and sale of a cake eyelash and eyebrow beautifier. The new product, named 'Maybelline', came in two shades: black (containing lamp black) and brown (containing iron oxides). It was sold for 75 cents and came in a small box with a picture of *The Maybell Girl* on the top.

The box included a rectangular cake of product stamped with the name Maybelline, a small bristle brush and a mirror attached to the inside of the lid. Its claim was that it was the 'ideal, harmless preparation for darkening eyelashes and eyebrows'.

In 1920, T L's decision to use the original name, Lash-Brow-Ine, came back to haunt him. He lost an appeal over a trademark dispute with Benjamin Ansehl of St Louis, Missouri. The loss meant that the business could no longer use the old name and cemented the use of 'Maybelline' in all advertising after that date.

> **SPARKPOINT:** *People watching is a great source of inspiration – what are they doing and why, and how could that be adapted or improved?*

45. LET THEM EAT TACOS

At the end of World War II, Glen Bell left the US Marine Corps and started his first hot dog stand in San Bernardino, California. Like many other new brands, he named it after himself – Bell's Drive-In. In 1952, he sold that stand and built a second, larger stand that sold hot dogs and hamburgers.

While he did reasonably well, two local brothers – who had also started out in the hot dog business but had similarly expanded to offer hamburgers, milk shakes and French fries – were providing stiff competition. The brothers were Richard and Maurice McDonald – yes, *those* McDonalds.

Glen decided he needed to find a different angle, and it didn't take him long. Looking across the street from his own restaurant he noticed long lines of customers at a Mexican restaurant, the Mitla Café, where they served tacos.

Investigating further, he learned that there were two reasons for the long lines. First, the tacos were very popular, and second, but slightly less positively, each taco took quite a long time to prepare and cook, so people had to wait around before getting their food.

Digging deeper still, he discovered that like most Mexican restaurants, the tacos at Mitla's began with soft flour tortillas that were filled first and then fried until crispy. Glen saw an opportunity for a fast food version if he could fry the shells in advance. This would mean that he and his teams would only need to stuff the shells, as they would be lined up and ready to go even before the store opened.

After some experimentation, he finally found a way to successfully deep-fry the shells in advance and opened his new taco stand – Taco Tia. His tacos sold for the princely sum of 19 cents.

Looking back on that day, Glen said: "I'll never forget the first taco customer, because naturally I was really concerned about his reaction. He was dressed in a suit and as he bit into the taco the juice ran down his sleeve and dripped onto his tie. I thought 'We've lost this one', but he came back, amazingly enough, and said, 'That was good; I'll take another one.'"

He opened three Taco Tias in the San Bernardino area but eventually sold those restaurants as he wanted to try out his concept in a bigger area: Los Angeles. He bought two lots on which he wanted to build his new restaurants, but was running short on capital and needed some partners. Those new partners included players from the Los Angeles Rams football team, who were fans of his Taco Tias.

He would go on to open four El Tacos in LA but still really wanted to go it alone – to have his name above the door – so sold his majority stake and opened his first Taco Bell in Downey, California, in 1962. This was quickly followed by eight more small stores.

In 1964, he sold his first franchise to an ex-policeman, and it too proved immensely successful. By 1967, just three years later, the company was opening its 100th restaurant. In 1978, the 868-location chain was sold to PepsiCo for $125 million in stock.

SPARKPOINT: *Inspiration and ideas aren't always about new products; they can help you to run the business better, to make it viable and profitable.*

46. MAKING AN INNOVATION OUT OF A CRISIS

As I sit writing this, my radio is on in the background and yet another group of politicians are discussing the latest developments in the ongoing saga that is Brexit. I find it quite hard to imagine how Brexit could be the inspiration for the birth not only of a new brand, but one that will go on to have true iconic status.

Yet, history tells us that a previous British constitutional crisis was just such an inspiration.

On 29 October 1956, Israel invaded the Egyptian Sinai and began what is known as the Suez Crisis, or the Second Arab-Israeli War. The Israeli invasion was quickly followed by incursions by the UK and France. The aim of the three allied countries was to regain control of the Suez Canal and to remove Egyptian President Gamal Abdel Nasser, who had recently nationalized the canal.

As the fighting started, an international crisis developed, and after a short period a combination of political pressure and financial threats from the US, the Soviet Union and the United Nations led to a withdrawal by the three invaders.

The episode humiliated the UK and France and strengthened Nasser. The British Prime Minister, Anthony Eden, resigned.

Another side effect of the crisis had been a reduction in the supply of petrol to the UK, which, in turn, had led to the government introducing petrol rationing. It was this rationing that was the inspiration that drove the rapid development of the car we know today as the Mini.

Alexander Issigonis was a former racing driver who became a successful engineer and designer. He had worked for Humber, Austin and Morris Motors Ltd when in 1955 he was recruited by British Motor Corporation's chairman, Sir Leonard Lord, to design a new range of three cars. The XC (experimental car) code names assigned for the new vehicles were XC/9001, for a large comfortable car, XC/9002, for a medium-sized family car, and XC/9003, for a small town car.

During 1956 Alexander had concentrated on the larger two cars, going as far as producing several prototypes.

However, at the end of 1956, following the introduction of the fuel rationing brought about by the Suez Crisis, Alexander was ordered by Lord to focus on bringing the smaller car, XC/9003, into production as quickly as possible.

Prototypes were running as early as 1957, and in August 1959 the car was launched simultaneously under British Motor Corporation's two main brand names, Austin and

Morris, as the Morris Mini Minor and the Austin Seven. (It wouldn't be until 1961 that it would be renamed the Austin Mini, and eight more years before the Mini became a marque in its own right.)

Alexander and his team were incredibly innovative with their design, introducing a space-saving transverse engine/front-wheel drive layout. This allowed 80% of the area of the car's floorpan to be used for passengers and luggage, contributing to its compact size and good fuel efficiency. It was an approach that would influence a generation of carmakers.

The car was an immediate and huge success and went on to become an icon of 1960s British popular culture, not least for a starring role in the 1969 film, *The Italian Job*.

Lovely though the story is, I am still struggling to see how the still-talking politicians and Brexit will be inspiration for anything as inventive and iconic as the Mini. But then again, I'm not sure I would have guessed the Suez Crisis would be inspirational either.

SPARKPOINT: *How can you take inspiration from a crisis?*

47. A MARKET ALL SOWN UP

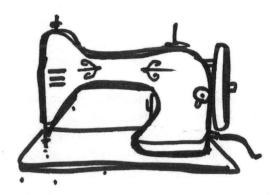

To try and sum up Isaac Merritt Singer is no easy task.

He was at different times an actor, machinist, carpenter, inventor, ruthless businessman, flamboyant salesman and the father of 24 children, courtesy of various wives and mistresses. His is also the name behind the most famous brand of sewing machine.

The Singers were a German immigrant family living in upstate New York when Isaac was born in 1811. He had minimal schooling but developed a real passion for the theatre. He took jobs as a labourer, carpenter and mechanic to fund his passion and worked as an actor whenever he could. He even tried running his own small theatre touring company, but it was unsuccessful.

He also found time to try inventing machines. One of those inventions was the first practical sewing machine for general domestic use. It was developed in an 11-day flurry of creativity and at the cost of the then princely sum of $40.

Isaac came across sewing machines while working for Orson C Phelps of Boston, who manufactured them under license from John A Lerow. The Lerow and Blodgett machines were not very practical; the circular movement of the shuttle took a twist out of the thread at every revolution.

He thought there was room for improvement. As he put it: "Instead of the shuttle going around in a circle, I would have it move to and fro in a straight line. In place of the needle bar pushing a curved needle horizontally, I would have a straight needle and make it work up and down."

He also introduced the idea of using a foot-driven treadle, similar to that of a spinning wheel, whereas all the other machines at the time used a hand crank to generate power.

Isaac's machine can't claim to be the first sewing machine. Indeed, its use of a lock stitch, which had been developed by Elias Howe, led to a patent battle that would only be settled after a few years in court and with the agreement of a patent-sharing accord among the major firms.

Isaac formed IM Singer & Company with New York lawyer Edward C Clark, and the first Singer sewing machines were offered for sale. True to his love of the theatre, Isaac decided to promote his invention himself and undertook a tour, demonstrating it at fairs and halls while giving heart-rending recitations of Thomas Hood's *Song of the Shirt*.

Within two years Singer was the leading manufacturer and marketer of sewing machines in the US.

The ongoing success, however, wasn't all down to Isaac's showmanship. In 1856 his business partner Edward starting offering a hire-purchase plan, the prototype for all instalment payment plans.

This meant that many of his potential customers, who couldn't afford the total cost at the point of purchase, could still become owners. The sales pitch was that they could increase their productivity, earn more money and improve their position in life … and afford the monthly payments and interest!

This arrangement did draw scrutiny, and *Scientific American* magazine reflected on the curious psychological fact that customers preferred to pay $100 in monthly instalments of $5, rather than the $50 the product cost, even though some of them had the money to buy one outright.

Nevertheless, people paid and business boomed.

Isaac stopped touring and hired female demonstrators to disprove any suggestions that women were too fluffy or incompetent to work a machine.

With no touring and with profits rolling in, Isaac had the funds to express his theatrical nature, and back in New York he took to driving about in a grand vehicle of his own design. It was painted canary yellow and black and was drawn by six horses. On board it had room for a small band to play, seats for 31 people and even a water closet.

His marital affairs and love life would have made an interesting show. He'd married for the first time at 29, but after a few years left his wife and their two children for a mistress with whom he'd go on to have 10 more children. If that weren't enough, he would set up two more households with women by whom he had another six children. In all, he fathered 18 offspring.

By 1860 the company was the world's biggest producer of sewing machines, but the increasing rows between his various partners and the growing interest of the press became so tiresome that Isaac decided to move to Europe. True to form, in 1863 he married his second wife, a Parisian boarding-house keeper named Isabella Boyer, and together they would have six more children.

He settled in England and built Oldway House at Paignton in South Devon, a palatial mansion large enough for him to have many of his children stay with him. It included his own private theatre, which he called The Wigwam.

Isaac died there in 1875, aged 63.

The Singer brand, however, lives on, though I doubt many of its users know the story of its founder.

SPARKPOINT: *Working in lots of different jobs can help you take a broader perspective on how to innovate.*

48. FIRING YOUR IMAGINATION

Back in 2004, hardware companies tended to be hardware companies, software companies were software companies and web companies were web companies. Retailers sold things other people made or produced. Most companies stayed close to their core, which was why Jeff Bezos' idea was so radical.

Amazon's goal of becoming 'the world's largest bookstore' had been achieved, but Jeff believed that selling and distributing books electronically would be a cost-effective practice and would further his aim to bring people to books.

So, in August that year, Jeff and his senior vice president of worldwide digital media, Steven Kessel, met Jateen Parekh and persuaded him to join Amazon as the first employee of Lab126, a new 'skunkworks' division. Jateen and a few industrial designers and engineers set up shop in an empty room in the offices of A9, Amazon's Palo Alto, California, subsidiary.

The team spent the first few weeks researching existing e-readers of the time, such as the Sony Librie, which required AAA batteries, sold poorly and never made it out of Japan. They concluded the market was still wide open. "It was the one thing that wasn't being done well by anyone else out there," said Jateen.

While Lab126 would be given nearly unlimited resources, Jeff's expectations were high. He wanted to fire up his new team, so he set a challenge that the new e-reading device needed to be drop-dead simple to use. He felt that having to continually configure devices to different Wi-Fi networks was too complicated for non-tech-savvy users, nor did he want to force customers to connect their device to a PC.

The simple sounding but technically difficult solution would require the team to build cellular access into the device, the equivalent of embedding a wireless phone in the hardware! Jeff didn't want customers to know there was a wireless connection or even pay for any access. "I thought it was insane," said Jateen. "I really did."

Not surprisingly, the first Kindle took more than three years to develop. As Steven, Amazon's digital media head, recalled: "Originally I told Jeff it would take us about 18 months to build the Kindle and we could do it with a couple of handfuls of folks. It took us three-and-a-half years and a lot more than a couple of handfuls of folks."

The Kindle, as it would be called, was finally launched in November 2007. It had a six-inch E Ink display and offered a free wireless connection over Sprint's EV-DO network.

There was no touch control, however, so the Kindle offered a full keyboard, navigation buttons and a quirky wedge-shaped design intended to make it easy to hold while typing. It also offered a speaker, headphone socket and expandable SD card storage.

It cost $399 and was only available in the US, offering access to 90,000 books at launch time.

The Kindle was showcased in *Newsweek* magazine, and to say it was an immediate success would be an understatement. It sold out within five-and-a-half hours. It would remain unavailable for five months as production caught up with demand.

The name Kindle was conceived by San Francisco designer Michael Cronan.

He didn't want it to be 'techie' or trite, but wanted something meaningful and memorable. One test for the new name would be that it worked as part of normal expressions, like, "I love curling up with my xxxxx to read a new book."

Inspiration in the end came from a suitably bookish source – a Voltaire quotation. "The instruction we find in books is like fire," the French novelist wrote. "We fetch it from our neighbours, kindle it at home, communicate it to others and it becomes the property of all."

The product's logo features a boy reading under a tree. While the imagery seems open to interpretation, the most likely explanation appears to be that the boy is sitting in the form of a letter 'K', standing for Kindle;

the tree (in versions where all of it is shown) resembles the shape of a human brain; and the boy is 'kindling' his imagination.

In short, it's all about enlightenment of the individual through reading.

Over the 10+ years that they've been around, Kindles have evolved considerably. And, as the Kindle's first product manager, Charlie Tritschler, said, there is still more to come: "Our ultimate dream is to get Kindle to be like a sheet of paper. Can we get the product thin and light enough – flexible and durable? We're not there yet, but we've made great progress and we are definitely not done."

Now there's a challenge to fire up your imagination.

SPARKPOINT: *Looking for new ways to deliver your brand's long-term vision or purpose can be a source of inspiration.*

49. TURNING INNOVATION ON ITS HEAD

In the US, 97% of households have at least one bottle of ketchup in the kitchen, yet the origin of the product is not American.

The word 'ketchup' is an Anglicized version of a Hokkien Chinese word, kê-tsiap, which is their name for a sauce derived from fermented fish. It is believed that British and Dutch traders first brought it back from Southeast Asia in the 1600s and started trying to replicate it.

These early attempts weren't like today's ketchup as they used ingredients like mushrooms, walnuts, oysters or anchovies in their efforts to reproduce the savoury taste. These sauces were mostly thin and dark, and were added to soups, sauces, meat and fish to enrich the flavours.

Tomatoes started being added in the early 1800s, probably first in the US due to a glut of tomatoes. These new recipes often included tomato pulp, spices and brandy, but still lacked the vinegar and sugar present in contemporary versions.

While the taste was closer to what we know today, preservation was often a problem. Some producers used poor quality tomatoes or even scraps, then handled and stored the product poorly, and the result was contamination from bacteria, spores, yeast and mould. This led to the use of many potential harmful preservatives.

At the end of 19th century, some argued that with better handling and ingredients, preservatives shouldn't be unnecessary. One of the leading exponents of this view, Dr Harvey Washington Wiley, teamed up with a Pittsburgh foodstuffs merchant named Henry J Heinz and developed a new ketchup recipe. It used ripe, red tomatoes – which have more of the natural preservative, pectin, than the scraps other manufacturers used – and dramatically increased the amount of vinegar.

This preservative-free ketchup was a huge success and soon dominated the market.

And everyone poured happily ever after? Well, not quite.

Despite the public's love of the taste of Heinz Ketchup, there were 'accessibility' problems that for years the brand didn't address. They stemmed from the gloriously rich, thick texture of the condiment and the resulting issue of pouring ... or rather *not* pouring.

People would hold the bottle at varying angles and slap its bottom, which led to splashes and splotches on shirts, blouses and table tops. Some people would even resort to inserting a knife into the bottle to loosen the ketchup. Rather than addressing the problem, Heinz tried to make light of it in their advertising by featuring people waiting for it to arrive or using slapping sounds.

It wasn't until 2002 that Heinz finally got around to doing something about the predicament, although the solution had been staring the company's researchers in the face for many years.

'Ethnographic research' is research that takes place *in situ*, in the natural habitat of whatever or whomever you are researching. In the case of Heinz Ketchup users, this meant in their homes.

What researchers had seen for years was that many consumers stored their ketchup bottles upside-down in their fridge or cupboard. Finally the penny dropped and someone suggested a really radical solution: How about an upside-down bottle?

Luckily for Heinz, recent developments in 'valve' technology meant that not only would the ketchup be dispensed quickly and easily from a well-designed upside-down bottle, but there would be no unpleasant side effects – no drips, no leaks and even no 'farting ketchup' sound.

The latest valves worked when the bottle's sides were pressed; this caused slits in the nozzle to open like flower petals and release the contents. When the pressing stopped the air was sucked back into the dome, causing it to retract and the slits to shut. A little grooved trap that ran around the cap collected any 'serum' and remixed it into dispensed ketchup as it came out, so that there was no watery, runny bit.

And as Wayne Cleary, Heinz's manager of packaging systems, explained, 'flatulence' is kept to a minimum because the upside bottle means, "The product is at the opening, if stored correctly. You're not waiting for the product to come down to the opening with the air and all."

The new format was launched in 2002, and it won packaging industry awards and consumer raves. Yet, as Patrick Macedo, Heinz's brand manager, wryly observed: "A lot of consumers were already storing their ketchup upside down. We just helped them do what they were already doing – better."

SPARKPOINT: *Not all innovations need to be radical – small changes can have big effects. What small changes could you make to help your brand?*

50. A FACTORY IN THE COUNTRY – INSPIRED BY YOUR PRINCIPLES

Quakers are a group with Christian roots that began in England in the 1650s. The formal name of the movement is the Society of Friends or the Religious Society of Friends.

There are two stories as to how the movement got its name.

The first says that the founder, George Fox, once told a magistrate to tremble (quake) at the name of God, and the name 'Quakers' stuck. The alternative theory is that the name derives from the physical shaking that sometimes accompanies Quaker religious experiences.

There is less controversy about where 'Friends' comes from. The general agreement is that it stems from the Bible, where in John 15.14 Jesus said: "You are my friends if you do what I command you."

There are a number of beliefs and principles that Quakers adhere to and, at the beginning of the 19th century, these included a prohibition against attending universities. This meant that Quakers could not pursue professions such as medicine and the law. Nor, as pacifists, could they consider military careers.

The result was that many Quakers started working in various trades. The Cadbury family was no exception, and moved from Exeter to set up and run a draper's shop in Birmingham.

When John Cadbury decided to follow his father into the trade, his decision was shaped by another principle of the Quakers, namely that they were teetotal and therefore keen to promote alternatives to alcohol. John chose to open a tea, coffee and drinking chocolate shop next door to his father's drapery in Bull Street.

He was soon to focus on cocoa, often grinding the beans himself, and by 1831 the shop devoted itself entirely to drinking chocolate.

By the 1850s John had been given a Royal Warrant from Queen Victoria, and in 1860 his sons George and Richard had taken over running the business. They imported a Dutch chocolate press and made something akin to what we would recognize today as a bar of chocolate.

Cadbury's Dairy Milk Chocolate was introduced in 1905. The recipe called for a higher percentage of milk than rival products, giving the confection a smoother taste and texture, and by 1914 it had become the company's best-selling item.

The success of the Cadbury brand meant that the brothers were soon very wealthy.

While not the first to produce chocolate, what they did with their wealth was quite different from their fellow chocolatiers. They were appalled by deplorable living standards in Birmingham, so instead of spending their riches on themselves George and Richard set out to fulfil their vision of creating a 'factory in the country'.

They bought a farm on the banks of the River Bourn and named it 'Bournville'. They built not only a huge factory but also hundreds of bright, airy homes with gardens and fruit trees for their workers. The village included open spaces, trees and public baths, but of course – reflecting the brothers' Quaker roots – no pubs. When Richard died in 1899, George placed the entire 1,000-acre community into a trust.

Today, many of its 25,000 residents still work for Cadbury and rent their homes from the Bournville Village Trust.

There are still no pubs in Bournville, and it's home to the only alcohol-free branch of the Tesco supermarket chain in Britain.

SPARKPOINT: *Limiting what you're looking for can sound counterproductive, but it can actually help focus the mind.*

51. FROM PORK CHOPS TO ICE POPS

That there is a connection between pork and ice cream might not be obvious until you say the name 'Wall's'. Even then, why one brand would choose to move from pork chops to ice cream isn't clear.

The story behind the decision begins in 1786 when Richard Wall opened a butcher's stall in St James's Market, London. Selling meat and meat products, he gained a reputation for being a very fine pork butcher. It took a while, but in 1812 Richard received the first of what would be a string of Royal Appointments. He duly became 'George, Prince of Wales' Purveyor of Pork' and continued to serve him through his later reign as King George IV.

In 1817 his son Thomas was born, followed in 1824 by his daughter, Eleanor. Richard's business boomed, and in 1834 he moved to new premises at 113 Jermyn Street. However, he died the same year, leaving his widow, Ann, and the 17-year-old Thomas to run the business, now trading as Ann Wall and Son.

There was more bad news when two years later, in 1836, Ann also died. Thomas had to take sole charge of the business, as well as the care of his 12-year-old sister.

The business continued to prosper, and there was other good news for the family as well. Thomas Wall II was born in 1846, to be followed not long afterwards by a second son, Frederick. They would both join their father in the family business, which was renamed Thomas Wall and Sons Ltd.

Throughout this time their skill and the quality of their produce remained top-notch, and Royal Warrants followed from Queen Victoria, King Edward VII and King George V.

One ongoing problem for the business was that it was very seasonal; in the summer, sales of meat, meat pies and sausages fell sharply and staff had to be laid off as a consequence.

Looking for inspiration, Thomas II thought about what sold well in the summer, and proposed developing a line of ice creams. It seemed like a great solution, but the world had other ideas, and the outbreak of World War I put the new initiative on hold.

Following Thomas II's retirement in 1920, the business was sold to MacFisheries and then to the Lever Brothers.

At Lever Brothers, Maxwell Holt was put in charge of the new acquisition, and while looking for new sources of growth he came across and revived the idea of producing ice cream, with near instant success.

Ice cream production commenced in 1922 at a factory in Acton. In 1959, Wall's doubled capacity by opening a purpose-built ice cream factory in Gloucester.

From Wall's pork meat to Wall's Funny Feet – from a meat feast to an ice cream feast – perhaps the connection isn't so strange after all.

SPARKPOINT: *Looking for solutions to gaps in your brand's performance can pay dividends.*

52. THE KEY TO A NEW INNOVATION

While the Industrial Revolution in the UK brought many improvements for the economy and life in general, there were a few less positive side effects. The rise of factory production helped give birth to the modern city, but with increased urbanization came an increased opportunity for crime.

An 1817 burglary in Portsmouth Dockyard, in which skeleton keys were used to unlock a door, proved to be the final straw for the government. It announced a competition to produce a lock that could be opened only with its own key, rendering it to all intents and purposes 'unpickable'.

Jeremiah Chubb, who was working with his brother Charles as a ship's outfitter and ironmonger in Portsmouth, decided to take up the challenge

Jeremiah's idea was based on the simple premise of a lock that would jam – it would essentially re-lock itself – if anyone tried to open it with anything other than the right key.

After many attempts, he finally developed and patented what became known as the 'detector lock' in 1818. It was a four-lever tumbler lock that when picked or opened with the wrong key would stop working until a special key was used to reset it. The security feature that jammed the lock was called a 'regulator' or 're-locker', and it not only stopped unauthorized access attempts, it indicated to the lock's owner that it had been interfered with.

The new lock won Jeremiah the £100 award that had been offered by the government, and it would be decades before anyone successfully managed to pick that original design.

Using this money, the brothers moved from Portsmouth to Wolverhampton, which soon became the lock making capital of England.

The business grew, and soon after the first-ever Post Office letterbox was fitted with a Chubb lock. In 1823 Chubb was awarded a special licence by George IV and went on to become the sole supplier of locks to the Post Office and to HM Prison Service.

When the priceless, world famous Koh-i-Noor diamond was put on display at the Great Exhibition of 1851, Chubb was commissioned to design a special security display cage.

The brand's fame and reputation for unpickable locks continued to grow. In the short story *A Scandal in Bohemia*, Arthur Conan Doyle had Sherlock Holmes describe a house with a "Chubb lock to the door".

In another Conan Doyle short story, *The Adventure of the Golden Pince-Nez*, Holmes asks, "Is it a simple key?" to which Mrs Marker, an elderly maid, replies, "No, sir, it is a Chubb's key."

The locks' identification as a Chubb, and the inference that they therefore could not have been picked, is a minor clue that leads Holmes to solve each of the stories' mysteries.

SPARKPOINT: *Though somewhat obvious, both competitions and the rewards they promise are great incentives for people to come up with new ideas.*

53. AN IDEA WORTH EVERY PENNY

Some people get paid to come up with ideas, although they don't necessarily get as much as you might expect for their innovations.

"We got £3,000 all-in for the creation of the world's most successful cream liqueur," recalled David Gluckman who, with his business partner Hugh Seymour-Davies, invented Baileys Irish Cream.

It is without doubt a phenomenally successful brand – the sale of the billionth bottle was celebrated on 3 December 2007 and it's likely that a further 250 million bottles have been sold since then, bringing the total up to approximately 1,250,000,000.

Given those astronomical numbers, £3,000 doesn't sound much, even if that's equivalent to £37,750 today.

However, according to David the original idea didn't take them too long.

"The initial thought behind Baileys Irish Cream took about 30 seconds," he said. "In another 45 minutes the idea was formed. Baileys was like that for me. A decade of experience kicked in and delivered a great idea."

David and Hugh, two former advertising executives, had formed the consultancy I&D (for Innovation & Development) and their first informal brief came courtesy of the beverage distributor IDV (International Distillers & Vintners).

The brief was pretty minimal: the Irish company within IDV wanted a new drinks brand for export.* They hadn't specified what kind of drink it should be, merely that it should be alcoholic. David remembers that they labelled the brief 'The Wexford Whisper'.

One day in, as the pair chatted about the 'Whisper', David – who'd been part of a team that had created the Kerrygold brand in the early 1960s – wondered if there was anything they could borrow from this previous Irish dairy experience.

"Is there something in Ireland's reputation for dairy produce that we can apply to an alcoholic drink – all those lush green, rain-sodden pastures and contented cows?" David wondered out loud. Hugh replied: "What would happen if we mixed Irish whiskey and cream? That might be interesting."

David and Hugh decided then and there that the best way to find out was to try it, and went straight to the nearest supermarket, what was the International Stores at the southern end of Berwick Street Market in the middle of Soho.

They bought a small bottle of Jameson Irish Whiskey and a tub of single cream and hurried back to the office. They mixed the two ingredients and tasted the resulting concoction. "It was certainly intriguing," David recalled, "but in reality, bloody awful."

They decided to keep trying, and as they added sugar the taste improved. But they still felt it was missing something. So they went back to the supermarket, where after a little browsing they spotted some Cadbury's powdered drinking chocolate and decided to try that.

The resulting mix surprised them. Not only did they think it tasted really good, but it seemed that the unlikely blend had the effect of making the drink taste stronger, more like a full-strength spirit.

The whole process had taken about 45 minutes.

David called Tom Jago, their client at IDV, and suggested that they meet immediately. Tom tried the product and instantly liked it.

The name Baileys also owed something to David's experience with Kerrygold. He and Hugh had thought that a family name might be better than a 'thing' or a place name, as many drinks were named after the people who made them.

However, David had been told during his Kerrygold days that some Irish names sounded overly quaint when applied to brands, so they decided they wanted an 'Anglo-Irish' name. Inspiration struck as the pair were out and about in Soho; alongside a pub called 'The Pillars of Hercules' in Greek Street was a restaurant bearing the name 'Baileys Bistro'.

The nascent brand still needed technical development, a bottle design and endorsement from the Irish team, all of which it duly got.

It was launched in 1974.

Baileys Irish Cream wasn't an overnight sensation, selling slowly but steadily at first. It would be another three years before it really began to take off, but once on its way there was no looking back.

SPARKPOINT: *There are some people who are very good at coming up with new ideas, so one source of 'inspiration' is to hire them or their services.*

---

* One of the reasons IDV were so keen on a new export brand was that the Irish management team had reached an agreement with the Irish finance minister that export earnings from the new product would be tax-exempt for a period of 10 years.

54. EVERY BRAND NEEDS A LITTLE LUCK

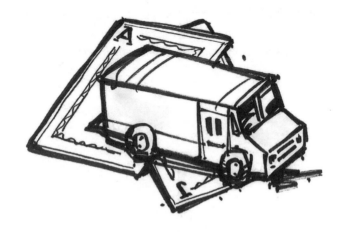

Frederick (Fred) Smith had the idea for FedEx while majoring in economics at Yale University in 1962. He even wrote about it for an end-of-term paper, though he never thought his tutors were that impressed.

Years later, when asked how the report went over, he admitted, "I don't know what grade; probably made my usual C."

What he had spotted and outlined in his paper was that the delivery companies of that time only transported large packages by truck or passenger planes. Fred thought it would be more efficient and profitable to carry small, but essential, urgently required items by airplane.

So, in 1971 Fred founded the company with $4 million of inheritance and $80 million in loans and equity investments. FedEx started out with eight airplanes, covering 35 cities, and it had plans to add more each month.

The first two years were incredibly tough, with unexpectedly high and steadily rising fuel costs. (This was, after all, the era of the OPEC oil embargo.) The company found itself millions of dollars in debt and on the brink of bankruptcy. Fred pitched the General Dynamics board for extra funding but was rejected. The company had to rely on pilots using their personal credit cards to fuel planes and requests to employees not to cash paychecks.

Funds continued to dwindle and soon there was only $5,000 left.

Fred had to do something drastic.

So what did he do? On an impulse, while waiting at an airport, he decided to change his plans and go to Las Vegas and play a little blackjack using the last $5,000.

The gods of marketing were clearly looking down on him and he won $27,000, enough to keep the business going a little longer. The gods, having taken a hand, decided to stick around and the business started to perform better and better.

Nowadays FedEx delivers more than 1.2 billion packages every year in over 220 countries, although few people know that it was saved by the turn of some cards. New brands certainly need a good idea ... and a little luck can come in handy too.

SPARKPOINT: *In a world where time is so important and valuable, a winning innovation often makes something faster.*

55. THE YOUNG TRACTOR MANUFACTURER AND THE SUPERSTAR SUPERCAR

Ferruccio was born into a family of grape farmers but he was more interested in nuts – nuts and bolts, that is. He had a natural affinity for mechanics. During World War II he served in the Italian Air Force, where he further developed his skills in all things mechanical.

After the war he returned home, where he immediately spotted the local farmers' need for agricultural machinery. He set about repurposing old military machines and vehicles into tractors and soon he had built a very successful business.

Perhaps not too surprisingly, given his love of things mechanical, he decided to spend some of his new wealth on his dream car. So it was that in 1958 he bought a new Ferrari and a few other luxury cars.

Ferruccio had a passion for his cars and driving them; he even tried his hand at racing them.

However, with his technical expertise he started to notice some weaknesses and faults in his Ferrari. It was very noisy and handling on the road left a lot to be desired, but most frustratingly it had an inferior clutch that often needed repairing.

Ferruccio decided to take his thoughts and his complaints to Ferrari and worked his way up to the automaker's founder, Enzo Ferrari. At the time Ferrari was the true superbrand in luxury sports cars, the gold standard, and Enzo, the head of the brand and the family, didn't want to listen to the thoughts and technical suggestions of a young tractor manufacturer.

When this somewhat blunt message was given to Ferruccio, he decided then and there that he would simply beat Enzo at his own game by building his own supercar.

No idle threat, as Ferruccio was none other than Ferruccio Lamborghini.

Just four months later, in October 1963, Ferruccio unveiled the Lamborghini 350 GTV at the Turin Motor Show and by the end of 1964 Lamborghini sold his first 13 cars (renamed the 350 GT).

The former tractor manufacturer is nowadays one of Ferrari's most formidable rivals.

SPARKPOINT: *Something that makes you angry can be a great source of inspiration and innovation.*

56. DON'T GET COLD FEET

LL Bean was a brand born out of cold feet, and only survived because the founder didn't get cold feet when he ran into problems.

Leon Leonwood Bean was an avid outdoorsman who lived and hunted in Freeport, Maine. One day, coming home again with cold, wet feet, he decided something had to be done about his hunting footwear. He wondered if he could combine traditional workman's waterproof rubber boots with something more functional and comfortable. He took his fledgling idea to a cobbler who he got to sew leather tops onto the bottom and soles of rubber galoshes.

When he set up LL Bean in 1912, it was a one-room operation selling a single product: his new Maine Hunting Shoe. Using clever targeting, he produced and sent a promotional flyer to everyone who held a Maine hunting license.

The material announced: "You cannot expect success hunting deer or moose if your feet are not properly dressed."

The mailing was a great success and he received 100 orders. He was off to a flying start.

Unfortunately, quality control on those first 100 orders was not very good and 90 of them were returned.

He didn't get cold feet and drop his idea. Instead, he did three things:

- First he refunded everyone's money.
- Second, he hired the US Rubber Company in Boston to help produce a better product.
- Third, he launched LL Bean's 100% satisfaction guarantee.

The business was soon back on track and Maine Hunting Shoes – or 'Duck Boots' as they came to be known – were selling well, attracting a famous clientele that included Babe Ruth, Franklin D Roosevelt and Ernest Hemingway.

In 1917, Leon launched his first retail store in his hometown of Freeport. Today the LL Bean retail campus includes the flagship store, which is open 24 hours a day, 365 days a year.* In 2015, the outlet attracted more than three million visitors.

SPARKPOINT: *Combining two things into one is a clever means of innovating.*

---

* The 24/7 store has been open continuously since 1951 with only four exceptions. In 1962 Maine changed its blue laws, which prohibited all commercial selling on Sundays, but a town vote later reinstated the store's open-door policy. Then, in 1963 it closed to honour the death of President John F Kennedy. It also briefly closed to mark the deaths of founder Leon Bean in 1967 and his grandson Leon Gorman in 2015.

57. WHAT YOU NEED TO DO TO LAUNCH A BRAND IS WATCH TV

"My father was a hopeless cook, but made the best popcorn. Together, we'd spend hours playing with flavours and ingredients, impatiently waiting for each kernel to pop, so we could try out our latest recipe," said Cassandra Stavrou, co-founder of the popcorn brand Propercorn.

In 2009, Cassandra was working in advertising and noticed that her colleagues were always hit by a mid-afternoon slump. "Everyone wanted a snack but all that was on offer was a rice cake, which is bland and boring, or a chocolate bar that's unhealthy," she said. "I noticed an opportunity for a snack that was tasty and good for you."

She wondered if popcorn might be the answer, and it was then that she remembered the popcorn maker her father had given her. "I still had it in the box and felt that was a nice extra bit of conviction I needed."

Cassandra experimented in her kitchen but couldn't get the results she wanted. She hoped to find a way to season the popcorn where each popped kernel was kept moving as the flavour was applied, ensuring an even coating on each piece.

She solved the need for movement by buying a cement mixer and lining it with stainless steel, but applying the flavour was still proving to be a problem. Until one night, that is, when she was watching an episode of *Top Gear* and inspiration struck.

"They would paint the cars with a special spray kit that gives the finest mist," Cassandra said, and she realized this might be the solution to her challenge. "I bought one online and used it to apply the oil to the popcorn."

Having got the product the way she wanted, she was faced with another problem – finding a UK manufacturer who could make it in the same way. "It took nearly two years," she said. "UK manufacturing wasn't set up to season popcorn the way I planned to, tumbling on a really large scale. I was also young, with no proven track record. I would turn up to industrial estates and the people there would basically tell me to go home."

It was around then that Ryan Kohn, a friend of her ex-boyfriend, came on board as co-founder. Ryan was at the time running his own property development firm.

Cassandra was in fact following the advice of another famous start-up entrepreneur, Richard Reed of Innocent Drinks fame. He had told her, "You don't have to do it on your own. It's good to be accountable to someone."

Ryan's mother pumped £30,000 into the business, and in October 2011 they launched Propercorn with four flavours, including Sweet & Salty and Sour Cream & Chive.

Their first customer was the café at Google's London office. Ryan had a friend who worked at Google, and he put the pair in touch with the chef. Out of the 48 snacks on sale, Propercorn proved the most popular. "That was the first stat we had, and we went to (London eateries) Leon, Chop'd and Benugo and told them," Ryan said. "It caught their attention."

The brand is now available at major UK retailers and growing fast. In 2017 the company sold three million bags of Propercorn a month.

SPARKPOINT: *New ideas may need new production techniques, and you may need to look for inspiration from other industries (or on television!).*

58. HE SOLD SEASHELLS

In the 1830s it became fashionable to use oriental shells for interior decoration, and shopkeeper Marcus Samuel started importing and selling them from his bric-a-brac shop in London's East End. It was the beginning of what would become one of the biggest brands in the world, although the future wasn't in selling shells.

By 1866, with the business in the care of his children, Sam and Marcus Jr, trading now included importing rice, silk, copper and chinaware and exporting machines and textiles to Japan and elsewhere in Asia. Following a visit to the Black Sea, Marcus became interested in oil, something he believed had a bright future even though at that time it was only used for lubricants and lighting.

They weren't the only people to see the future potential; the Rothschilds were making huge investments in tunnels and railways in an attempt to begin moving oil by land. The reason for their strategy was that, at the time, transportation by sea was proving to be difficult due to spillage and weight.

The Samuel brothers, however, decided to go with what they knew through the family's history of international trading – sea transportation – but with a twist. They would transport by sea, though not in barrels as others did. They would ship in bulk, using tankers. They would also be the first brand to transport oil via the Suez Canal.

Their potentially risky strategy paid off.

The benefits proved to be threefold: not only could they transport more oil at once, they reduced leakage and were able to sell at a cheaper price. The brothers called their new oil transport company The Tank Syndicate.

Business was booming, and things got better quickly because by 1886 the combustion engine was being manufactured and distributed around the world. Around the same time, Karl Benz had introduced the Mercedes automobile, which had a four-stroke internal combustion engine.

These were the two engineering developments that would exponentially drive the demand for oil.

The company's name was changed again in 1897, this time to the Shell Transport and Trading Company, and in this new guise its operations were expanded to the Far East.

Here it would find itself in competition with the Royal Dutch Petroleum Company, a fierce battle that would continue until 1903, when both companies were faced with the increasing threat of the much larger Standard Oil. It was then that they formed a partnership that would be called the Asiatic Petroleum Company. In 1907, the company became Royal Dutch Shell, with Royal Dutch owning 60% and Shell Transport and Trading Company owning 40%.

However, the logo of the new company reflected its humble beginnings, first featuring a mussel shell image but later moving to the now iconic scallop shell.

SPARKPOINT: *Inspiration can come from trend watching; the bigger the trend, and the earlier you spot it, the better it is likely to be for you.*

59. PIECING TOGETHER THE JIGSAW OF AN IDEA

Sometimes getting to a new idea is a bit like making a jigsaw puzzle – there are lots of pieces you have to put together in order to see the final picture.

In Will Shu's case, his jigsaw led him to spot a first-world solution to a first-world problem, and one that he knew was growing fast.

Will liked his food. In fact, it was his passion, and his recommendation to all budding entrepreneurs is: "Do something that you actually care about personally."

The next piece of the puzzle came from his own experience. He'd started his working life as an investment banking analyst at Morgan Stanley in Manhattan, often putting in 80-100 hours a week. He could at least rely on getting good food to see him through those gruelling times:

"In New York, even in 2001, before internet orders, every restaurant delivered at every hour – that was a given."

However, when he was transferred to the firm's Canary Wharf office in London, in 2004, he found things were very different. "It was frustrating," he said. "I mean, it was definitely a first-world problem, but I was working similar hours and I got sick of going to Burger King."

The picture was becoming clearer: "I was like, wow … it would be great if I could change this."

Thinking about it more, Will realized that the 21st-century 'vice' of laziness wasn't a problem but an indication of the scale of the opportunity. "I think people are inherently lazy. I know I am," he said. "I view Deliveroo as one of those things where you're tired from a long day's work, you've gone home, and you're just like – I can't be f***ed. There'll also be people on their eighth hour of video games who just can't be bothered to get up. We're not going to discriminate against someone's laziness."

Another piece of the puzzle was Will's realization that while some local restaurants did make deliveries, the higher-end establishments could only host a certain number of sittings per night, which limited their revenue opportunity. These restaurants would be his 'supply chain' and his point of difference.

The final piece lay in technology advancements that would allow quick and easy ordering and tracking.

The jigsaw had come together. "Literally, I just wanted to create a company to deliver great food quickly," said Will. "That was really it. I didn't have any other ideas."

And so was born the idea of Deliveroo – an online platform that lets users order from quality restaurants that would ordinarily be out of reach due to limited bookings or travel distance, with food delivered to your door in 30 minutes.

Like many innovations, it sounded simple enough but would prove much more difficult to put into practice.

The start-up needed to create its own fleet of deliverers (or 'deliveroos', as it likes to call them) and an app, as well as behind-the-scenes infrastructure that could locate the best-placed delivery person to handle each order.

It also initially took some convincing to get higher-end restaurants to sign up with the service.

With initially limited funds, Will had to do lots himself, from pitching to restaurants to making deliveries. "At first, I didn't really have a choice – it wasn't like I decided to do it," Will said, referring to the eight months he spent as a delivery driver when he'd first launched Deliveroo back in 2013. "I funded it with my own money in the beginning, so you just do everything."

But five years on, and now sitting at the helm of the $2 billion company that operates in 84 cities, Will still likes to keep close to things.

"I still do deliveries once every two weeks," he said. "You get to really understand what restaurateurs are thinking, what customers are thinking, what drivers are thinking. I've done every job in the company. I think it's invaluable."

SPARKPOINT: *In Will's own words, "Do something that you actually care about personally."*

Footnote: Will thinks he is his own company's No. 1 customer: "I order from Deliveroo on average 1.7 times a day. That said, on Fridays I might order lunch for everyone in the office from 15 places, so maybe that makes me look a little gluttonous."

60. IT'S NO USE CRYING OVER SPILT CHOCOLATE

There is a saying in marketing that it isn't a problem, it's *an opportunity*, which shows what an optimistic bunch of people marketers are.

While that's not always the case, there is a bit of truth in the notion ... and so it was for Cadbury.

It was the 1920s and one of the machines in the Cadbury chocolate factory in Bourneville was acting up again, spilling folds of overflowing chocolate down its sides. Instead of just getting annoyed, the machine's operator noticed that the folds were setting as they cooled into a very soft and flaky texture.

He pointed it out to his manager, who told the people in marketing. They weren't interested in the problem but wondered instead if this presented an opportunity.

They decided to send some of the rippling, layered chocolate out for market research and see if they had stumbled across something.

Those initial results weren't too promising, to say the least. They were in fact awful, with people complaining that the chocolate was too soft and the bars literally fell apart when they opened the wrapper.

The most obvious response to such negative feedback would have been to scrap the idea. However, the marketers by now believed that there was something to the product – it was different from everything else on the market and they loved it.

So, they thought about why this delicious product wasn't better liked. They wondered if it was due to the 'shock of the new', a negative reaction that was triggered because people had certain expectations, resulting in the rejection of non-conforming, radical things. At the time, the widespread belief shaped by all the other products on the market was that a good chocolate bar was a smooth, solid, squared-away thing that didn't crumble or flake.

The Cadbury team decided to try again, but this time they would position the product very differently by making a virtue out of its crumbliness. They re-introduced it as the 'crumbliest, flakiest milk chocolate in the world'.

Since the 1930s Cadbury has been selling half-length Flakes specifically for prodding into vanilla soft serve ice cream in a cone, creating what is known as a '99'.

In the 1970s Cadbury Ireland created a variation on the flake – a Twirl – a crumbly, flaky bar very similar to a Flake but coated and held together in smooth milk chocolate. A white chocolate version of this was launched in 2000 and was called a Snowflake.

It worked. The brand launched nearly 90 years ago is still going strong … or rather, it's still crumbling and flaking all over the place.

SPARKPOINT: *When something goes wrong it can be the source of new ideas.*

Footnote: There are lots of stories about why the Flake bars made for dipping into ice cream are called 99s, often relating to ice cream stores at '99 something road'. However, the Cadbury website says the origin of the name isn't definitively known.

61. THE GLUE THAT WOULDN'T STICK

Perhaps one of the most famous of brand innovation stories starts with a failure.

Dr Spencer Silver, a 3M research scientist, was charged with developing a new, super-strong glue for use on one of the company's adhesive tapes.

After months of work he developed a new adhesive, but rather than being super-strong it proved to be super-weak!

The formulation of his new glue meant that the adhesive formed itself into tiny spheres, each with a diameter of just a paper's width. Each sphere was sticky but they only made intermittent contact with other surfaces. This meant that when the glue was coated onto the tape, the tape didn't stick very strongly. In fact, it could be peeled off quite easily.

While it was an unusual new adhesive, it wasn't what Spencer had been briefed to create and the project went into limbo. It was occasionally discussed but not actively developed.

It would be another four years before a practical use was found for it, and another six years before it came to market.

The man who found that breakthrough use – the 'killer app' – was another 3M development researcher named Arthur Fry.

He found the ideal use not at work, but when pursuing one of his hobbies. Arthur regularly sang in his church choir, and used scraps of paper as markers to keep his place in his hymnal, but was frustrated that they kept falling out. He heard about the new glue while attending an internal 3M seminar, in which Dr Silver, who was still championing the adhesive, espoused the virtues of the discovery.

Arthur was intrigued and wondered if this might be the answer to his prayers. He came up with the concept of a novel sort of bookmark: one that would keep its place and not fall out, but which could be removed without marking or damaging the paper to which it had been stuck.

The 3M Post-it Note was born.

Today, Post-its are sold in more than 100 countries.

SPARKPOINT: *New technology alone isn't enough – it needs an application that people can truly value.*

62. WHEN ONE USAGE ISN'T ENOUGH

Why settle for one usage when you could have two?

Sometimes it might be easier to stick with what you do well, but it's worth continually looking at how you could do things better or even use what you make in different ways.

So it was for Kutol's Wallpaper Cleaner. Never heard of it? I'm not too surprised, but I think you might know what it became.

The story begins in the 1930s in Cincinnati, Ohio, when soap maker Noah McVicker was asked by a client, Kroger Grocery, for a product that could clean coal residue from wallpaper. Noah created the new substance out of flour, water, salt, boric acid and mineral oil. It looked a bit like putty.

What made it so good was that it didn't contain any toxic chemicals, so it could be reused and did not stain the surface. In addition, it was sticky enough to pick up dirt and coal residue but not so sticky as to tear or otherwise damage wallpaper.

Noah's family soap company, Kutol Products, decided to market this creation as the ultimate wallpaper cleaner.

It was a reasonable success and everyone lived happily ever after. Well, not quite.

Things changed after World War II when there was a transition from coal-based home heating to natural gas, and a resulting decrease in internal soot. The introduction of washable vinyl-based wallpaper further exacerbated the situation and the market for wallpaper cleaning putty.

Luckily it was about this time that Noah's nephew, Joseph McVicker, joined the company. Joseph's sister-in-law, Kay Zufall, was a nursery school teacher and she had seen a newspaper article about making art projects with wallpaper cleaning putty. She tried it out with the children in her class and they loved it.

She told Joseph and together they sold the idea to the family company. The product was slightly modified so the detergents were removed and a pleasant scent and food colouring, all non-toxic, were added.

Originally, they were going to call the new plaything 'Rainbow Modelling Compound', but Kay hated the name. And so she and her husband came up with an alternative, more kid-friendly name: Play-Doh.

The new product was an immediate success.

In 1956, the McVickers started the Rainbow Crafts Company to make and sell Play-Doh. Macy's in New York and Marshall Field's in Chicago began carrying the product. The new company also began to advertise on popular children's television shows, such as *Captain Kangaroo*. Within one year its sales had already reached almost $3 million!

Today, Play-Doh is owned by Hasbro, which continues to make and sell the product through its Playskool line. In 2003, the Toy Industry Association added Play-Doh to its 'Century of Toys List', which contains the 100 most memorable and creative toys of the last 100 years.

> **SPARKPOINT:** *Finding a new use for an existing product, with or without minor modification, can be a source of innovation.*

63. MAKE IT BETTER

Michelin's history starts with a Dunlop tyre – a punctured one.

In October 1887, Scottish veterinarian and inventor John Boyd Dunlop developed the first practical pneumatic tyre. It started as a labour of love for his son's tricycle, but when he tested his inflated tube of sheet rubber against the old metal wheels he soon saw the potential.

When he rolled both across his yard, the metal wheel quickly stopped rolling but the inflated tube continued until it hit a gatepost and rebounded.

Dunlop decided to move on to larger tyres for full-size bicycles, and was granted a patent in December 1888.*

The new tyres quickly became popular among cyclists of the day, as they were far superior to the solid tyres that were in standard use.

Meanwhile, in Clermont-Ferrand, France, the brothers Édouard and André Michelin were running a rubber factory. They had made a small foray into the world of transportation innovation when they developed and introduced a rubber brake for cars, which at the time had wooden wheels.

One day, a local cyclist whose pneumatic Dunlop tyre needed repair turned up at the factory. Like all Dunlop tyres, it was glued to the rim. It took over three hours to remove and repair the tyre, which then needed to be left overnight to dry.

The next morning, Édouard inflated the tyre, fitted it back onto the wheel and took the bike out into the factory yard to test it. After only a few hundred metres, the tyre failed again. It would be another day before it was once again repaired and the cyclist would get his bike back.

Édouard was still enthusiastic about the pneumatic tyre – he could see all the advantages but realized that it would be so much better if it were easier and quicker to repair. So, he and his brother worked on their own version that did not need to be glued to the rim, and they created and patented the first removable pneumatic tyre. It had a special rim and tyre combination that worked with small bolts and clamps holding the two bits together, known as The Clincher. This meant that repairs could now be made in just 15 minutes.

It was a big success and was soon being adopted by enthusiasts and racers alike.

Charles Terront chose to use the new Michelin tyres for his attempt to win the Paris-Brest-Paris classic, a 1,200 km ride. Unfortunately, he had a puncture early on, but with nearby technicians he was able to make a quick repair and got going again.

Charles went on and won the race, which proved to be great publicity for the new tyres. The performance benefits were obvious to all: a rider had suffered fewer punctures, and when he did the repairs were much easier.

The Michelin brothers decided to capitalize on this, and organized a race from Paris to Clermont-Ferrand. To make things more interesting (and wanting to promote their product), they scattered nails across parts of the road.

Michelin still manufactures tyres for bikes but nowadays it also makes them for trains, planes, cars and even space shuttles. In 2012, the group produced 166 million tyres.

SPARKPOINT: *Can you do what someone else does but do it better?*

---

* John Dunlop wasn't actually the first to invent the pneumatic tyre. Unbeknown to him, another Scot, Robert William Thomson from Stonehaven, had patented a pneumatic tyre in 1847.

64. THE BILLION-DOLLAR BUTT

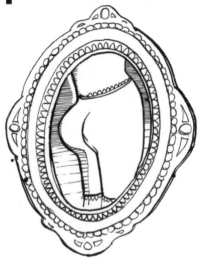

Sara Blakely may be the only woman in the world who's actually grateful for cellulite and back fat. They ended up being the reason behind her drive to turn $5,000 she'd saved from selling fax machines into a $250-million-a-year business.

When she's asked where the idea for her business came from, she says with delightful honesty: "My inspiration was my own butt."

Working in the hot Florida climate, Sara disliked the appearance of the seamed foot on her pantyhose, especially when she wore open-toed shoes, but she liked the fact that the control-top of the pantyhose eliminated panty lines and made her behind appear firmer.

When cutting the bottom off normal pantyhose didn't work (the cut-off edge on the legs rolled up too much), she started a search for the right material. Eventually coming upon a solution in a craft store, she wrote her own patent following instructions from a Barnes & Noble textbook and incorporated her company under the name 'Spanx'.

Not only candid, she was clearly committed to her cause. Once she'd had her first samples made, she looked up companies in the Yellow Pages to find potential retailers. Having identified Neiman Marcus as exactly the sort of store she wanted to sell Spanx, she set off to convince one of the department store's buyers of the merits of her new 'shapewear'.

Sara believes in the power of a product demonstration, and it wasn't long before she was in a Neiman Marcus restroom showing off her inspirational butt, demonstrating what it looked like before and after putting on Spanx.

It was a demonstration that got the brand its first listing, although initially in only seven Neiman Marcus stores.

When an excited Sara told the Spanx sample manufacturer about the Neiman Marcus deal, his response wasn't quite the one she'd been expecting. He clearly wasn't as convinced that this was the beginning of something big. Sara recalls him saying, "I thought these were just going to be Christmas gifts for the next five years."

She was, however, determined that Spanx was going to be a success, and she wasn't going to leave anything to chance. She started to call up everyone she knew who lived near those first Neiman Marcus stores and asked them to buy a pair of Spanx, promising that she'd reimburse their money. Her reasoning was that if they sold well there the chain would extend their distribution.

Yet it was still taking time to convince them. "Right when I was running out of friends and money," Sara and Spanx got their lucky break. "Oprah named them as one of her favourite things," she said.

That changed everything. Distribution spread quickly to Bloomingdales, Saks and Bergdorf Goodman. In 2001 she signed a contract with QVC, the home-shopping network, where she sold 8,000 pairs in the first six minutes.

Sara is now the world's youngest female self-made billionaire, according to *Forbes* magazine.

And I can almost hear her saying she is the lady with the first billion-dollar butt.

SPARKPOINT: *If your new idea to going to be sold through retail channels, a good start can be essential.*

65. IT TAKES ALL SORTS

It was 1899 in Sheffield, England, and salesman Charlie Robertson was making his pitch.

"Would you like a sandwich made of two layers of pink, orange, brown or white candy with a black, liquorice-flavoured layer in the middle?

"Perhaps you might prefer a double-decker sandwich made of white sweet paste and black liquorice layers.

"More exotic is our short cylinder of pink or yellow, coconut-flavoured candy that surrounds a central black, liquorice-flavoured cylinder.

"An elegant choice is our long, thin, black, liquorice-flavoured cylinder surrounding a cylinder of white candy.

"If you're a true liquorice lover you could have a long, black, solid cylinder of liquorice-flavoured candy.

"If not, why not our flat, circular pink or blue candies covered with little balls and surrounding a gelatinous, anise-flavoured interior?"

Charlie was getting worried. His pitch wasn't going well.

He had been through almost the entire Bassett's portfolio of sweets and his potential client hadn't seemed interested in a single one.

Exasperated, he turned around to get his last few samples, but in doing so he knocked over a number of his jars.

His potential client took one look at the resulting higgledy-piggledy mixture of all the different sorts of liquorice-based sweets, and much to Charlie's surprise and great delight he immediately placed a large order for the mix.

Bassett's Liquorice Allsorts were born.

SPARKPOINT: *Variety may not only be the spice of life, but of innovation too. Sometimes more might be more.*

66. **LOVE IT OR HATE IT**

Marmite is a very particular old British brand, and more recently a term for something that divides opinion.

Marmite is a sticky, dark brown food paste with a distinctive, powerful and extremely salty flavour. It is mostly used as a spread on bread, toast and crackers, and often as a complement to cheese. It is in the same 'family' as Australian Vegemite, the Swiss Cenovis and the German Vitam-R.

The design on the front of the pack features a large, covered earthenware cooking pot that the French call a *marmite* – hence the name.

More recently the distinctive taste inspired a popular advertising campaign based on the idea that you either 'Love it or hate it'. Its divisive nature is such that the word

Marmite has entered everyday language as a metaphor for something that polarizes opinions.

However, this British institution with its French-inspired name owes its origin to a German and a by-product that was traditionally just thrown away.

A 19th century German chemist named Justus von Liebig had discovered by accident that brewer's yeast could be boiled, concentrated and then eaten, but nothing was done commercially with the substance in the UK.

That changed in 1902 when a group of British businesses recognized that in the capital of British brewing, Burton, large quantities of brewer's yeast were regularly thrown away. They decided to try and put some of it to good use, and taking the yeast from the largest brewery, Bass, they founded the Marmite Food Company. It was an immediate hit, and by 1907 it had become successful enough to warrant construction of a second factory at Camberwell Green in London.

A further boost to the brand came in 1912 with the discovery of vitamins and their health benefits. Marmite is a rich source of the vitamin B complex.

The vitamin B1 deficiency known as beriberi was common during the early part of the 20th century, which helped the brand, as did the fact that during World War I British troops were issued Marmite as part of their rations.

The brand is now owned by Unilever and continues to divide opinion wherever it goes, but its ongoing success proves that you don't have to appeal to all of the people all of the time.

SPARKPOINT: *Can you turn someone else's by-product into something valuable in its own right?*

67. THE GODFATHER OF GOOD COFFEE AND HIS THREE ADOPTED SONS

Einstein said, "Genius is 1% inspiration, 99% perspiration." The same could be said of innovation, although if you can build on someone else's blood, sweat and tears, then perhaps you won't need to contribute so much of your own perspiration.

The success of one of the world's most famous brands was built on the perspiration and generosity of the less-well-known Alfred H Peet.

Alfred was born in 1920. His father owned B Koorn & Company, which sold coffee, tea and spices in the Dutch city of Alkmaar, and his uncle ran the Keijzer coffee business in Amsterdam. Alfred's father thought his son might pursue a university education and do something scholarly, but coffee was in his blood. He quit school to become a 'coffee-man'.

His career was interrupted by World War II, when like lots of Dutchmen Alfred was forced to go and work in a German factory. After the war he returned to the beverage business.

He worked in London, Java and around New Zealand. In Java, he learned all about deep roasting coffee beans so that they released richer flavour. He found New Zealand boring and decided he wanted to try his luck in a faster-paced environment. And so, in 1955 he arrived in San Francisco.

He was appalled by the coffee in the US. "I came to the richest country in the world, so why are they drinking the lousiest coffee?" he asked himself.

Having done numerous jobs to raise the necessary capital, he opened up his own store: Peet's Coffee Tea & Spices. It was and is still on the corner of Vine Street and Walnut Street in Berkeley, California.

The store was a success and became a popular hangout for students at the nearby University of California campus, who loved the coffee and the slightly eccentric, 'old world' persona of the owner. They become known as 'Peetniks' (it was after all the height of the Beatnik era) and he was soon being called 'the godfather of quality coffee'.

In 1970, three friends who'd first met at the University of San Francisco – English teacher Jerry Baldwin, history teacher Zev Siegl and writer Gordon Bowker – were seeking a consultant to advise them on starting a quality coffee shop in Seattle. They heard about Alfred and his Peet's Coffee business and made the first of many visits to Berkeley.

A strong bond was formed almost immediately, and many believe Alfred saw the trio not just as his pupils but as the sons he never had. He was clearly flattered that three young men had come all the way to Berkeley to learn from him so they could start a company in Seattle. In the course of the next few weeks they learned how Alfred ran his business and Jerry learned how to roast coffee.

The business they went on to found was, of course, Starbucks and its original coffee supplier was, of course, Peet's.

As Jerry was to recall some years later, "He (Alfred) generously shared with us how to cup, to roast and to blend, and instilled his uncompromising standards. I'll always be in his debt."

Alfred's business expanded to include 150 stores in 10 states. Starbucks built on his inspiration and perspiration, and now has over 15,000 stores all around the world.

SPARKPOINT: *Finding and using a mentor can help you learn and avoid problems, but they are also a source of valuable inspiration.*

68. ACCIDENTS WILL HAPPEN, BUT THEN SO CAN INNOVATIONS

One measure of success for a brand is for it to acquire a nickname.

Dr Martens doesn't have one. It has at least four – Doc Martens, Docs, DMs and Bovver boots – and even the soles, which are trademarked as AirWair, are known colloquially as Bouncing Soles.

It is a British brand but the original inspiration came from a German orthopaedic surgeon.

Klaus Märtens was a doctor in the German army during World War II. While on leave in 1945, he went skiing in the Alps but unfortunately took a spill and injured his ankle. It caused a lot of pain and he found that his standard-issue army boots, and even ordinary shoes, were just too uncomfortable.

He had to find a solution, and started work on ways to improve the comfort of his boots. Inspiration came from seeing some tyres and he landed on the idea of air-padded soles.

After the war Klaus started making and selling the boots, but without much success. Luckily for him, about this time he met up with an old university friend, Herbert Funck, who had become an engineer.

Herbert was intrigued by the new shoe design, and the two decided to go into business together. In 1947, in Seeshaupt, Germany, they started producing a revised and improved boot, using discarded rubber from old Luftwaffe planes and airfield equipment.

The comfortable soles were a big hit with German housewives, and about 80% of sales in the first decade were to women over the age of 40.

In 1952 they opened a factory in Munich, and by the end of the '50s – looking for new sources of growth – they started exploring opportunities to market the foot-wear internationally.

British shoe manufacturer R Griggs Group Ltd. were immediately interested and agreed to buy patent rights to manufacture the shoes in the UK.

The company decided to anglicize the name to Dr Martens. They slightly re-shaped the heel to make the shoes fit better and, showing their flair for branding, added what would be the trademark yellow stitching. They took out the British trademark on the soles as 'AirWair'.

Launched on April Fool's Day in 1960, the first Dr Martens boots in the UK were the 1460 model, a style that's still in production today. They featured an eight-eye-let, oxblood-coloured, smooth leather design.

Sales quickly proved that it hadn't been a foolish decision to buy the patent rights. The immediate appeal was among people who were on their feet a lot and wanted the extra comfort – postmen, policemen and factory workers.

However, as time passed the brand started to appeal to other groups of people. In the 1960s, skinheads started to wear what they called 'DMs'. In the late 1970s they became popular among punks, new wave musicians and other youth subcultures.

In 2006, Griggs' 1960 Dr Martens AirWair boot was included in the Design Museum/BBC list of British design icons, along with the Concorde, Mini, Jaguar E-Type, Aston Martin DB5, Supermarine Spitfire, Tube map, World Wide Web and the AEC Routemaster bus.

SPARKPOINT: *Surprisingly, personal misfortune or injury can be a source of inspiration.*

69. A LITTLE BIT OF QUALITY FOR EVERY STREET

The fashion for using local products is nothing new.

In 1890, when John Mackintosh and his wife opened a shop in Halifax, they created a new kind of sweet by mixing hard toffee with runny caramel. It was made from inexpensive local ingredients such as milk, beet sugar and eggs.

In 1898 they expanded the operation with construction of the world's first toffee factory. When John died in 1920, his son Harold inherited the business.

Business continued to thrive, but in the early 1930s Harold decided he wanted to create something new and different.

At the time only the wealthy could afford boxed chocolates, as they were made from exotic ingredients from around the world and had elaborate packaging that often cost as much as the chocolates themselves.

Harold's idea was that what was good enough for the wealthy was good enough for everyone, and he set out to produce boxes of chocolates that could be sold at a reasonable price. To him an obvious place to start was cutting the cost of the elaborate packaging. He decided that he'd create a selection of different toffees covered with chocolate and present them in low-cost yet attractive boxes.

The packaging would be much less costly because rather than having each chocolate separated in the box, Harold planned on individually wrapping them in coloured paper and putting them into a decorative tin. To achieve this, he would introduce a new technology: the world's first twist-wrapping machine.

He wanted to create a wonderful multi-sensory effect the whole family could enjoy – when the tin was opened a chocolate aroma would burst out and there would be a visual feast of different textures, colours, shapes and sizes of wrapped sweets.

The product still needed a name and some imagery, and while current brand owner Nestlé claim it isn't related, there do seem to be striking similarities with a play by JM Barrie, the author of *Peter Pan*.

The official story is that Harold recognized that Britain in the mid- to late-1930s was still feeling the effects of the Great Depression, and that in times of economic hardship people often look back to 'the good old days', craving nostalgia. He therefore decided to feature two quaint characters named Miss Sweetly and Major Quality. The brand would be called Quality Street.

Now it so happens that *Quality Street* is also the name of the play written by Barrie. It is a comedy about the relationship between Captain Valentine Brown, Miss Phoebe Throssel and Miss Livvy, a more energetic, flirtatious and naughty version of her younger self that Phoebe invents and plays to tease Captain Brown. The play is set in Napoleonic times, with the characters in old-fashioned dress.

The original Broadway production opened in 1901 and ran for only 64 performances. The show was then produced in London, where it was a hit, running for 459 performances. It was frequently revived until World War II.

Whatever the true origin of the name and the characters, the brand was and is a huge success.

The numbers tell the tale: 6,000 Quality Street sweets are produced per minute, for a total of 67 million every week; 136,701 miles of foil are used per year to wrap the candies, the equivalent distance of five times around the equator; and 15 million tins of Quality Street were sold in 2010, enough to stretch to the moon and back if placed end to end.

SPARKPOINT: *Democratizing something that has traditionally been a premium product can deliver big rewards.*

Footnote: These were the original 18 varieties, as described by Lord Harold Mackintosh:

1. Chocolate Crème Toffee Brazils (now called The Purple One)
   Inside the moulded chocolate is a Brazil nut embedded in a lovely rich toffee, which is as soft as a fondant.

2. Café Au Lait Carameline
   Similar in character to the 'Cup', but the toffee centre is blended with milk and coffee.

3. Toffee Cup (now called the Caramel Swirl)
    A moulded chocolate with an 'almost liquid' toffee centre –
    Toffee Cup truly describes it.

4. Noisette Pate (now called the Green Triangle)
    A layer of finely ground nuts in a chocolate paste, moulded with
    a layer of chocolate of exceptional smoothness.

5. Milk Chocolate Whirl
    Made with a delicious milk chocolate paste.

6. Jaffa Chocolate Toffee
    A unique combination of sultanas mixed with toffee and covered
    with orange milk chocolate.

7. Quality Street Toffee
    A plain toffee from a new recipe; very rich in cream.

8. Almond Toffee
    The same delicious toffee combined with finely chopped almonds.

9. Chocolate Toffee Crispets
    A combination of a crisp cereal and toffee coated with chocolate.

10. Valencia Cracknel
    The choicest of almonds in the usual cracknel casing.

11. Quality Street Extra Butter Toffee (now called the Toffee Penny)
    Made in the same way as Quality Sreet Toffee but with more butter -
    the name aptly describes it.

12. Quality Street Almond Extra Butter Toffee
    The same toffee with an almond on top.

13. Quality Street Harrogate Toffee
    The new toffee recipe with distinctive lemon and ginger flavour.

14. Chocolate Butter Toffee
    The same recipe as Quality Street Extra Butter Toffee,
    but chocolate coated.

15. Chocolate Butter Toffee Walnut
    Again, the same toffee but with a walnut added and the
    combination covered with superfine chocolate.

16. Quality Street Cream Caramel
    A new, rich and creamy soft-eating caramel.

17. Quality Street Vanilla Toffee
    Another special toffee recipe with a delicate vanilla flavour.

18. Golden Ingots (now called the Toffee Finger)
    Another variety of Chocolate Toffee in finger shapes.

70. WHY HAVE MILK WHEN YOU CAN HAVE 'CREAM'?

John Harvey & Sons can trace its origins back to a small family wine merchant established in 1796. It was owned originally by William Perry, who later went into partnership with Thomas Urch. Then in 1822 Thomas' nephew, John Harvey, joined the firm as an apprentice.

John rose swiftly through the ranks and by 1839 he was senior partner in the Bristol branch. By 1871 the whole business was known as John Harvey & Sons. Its trade was based mainly on Spanish and Portuguese wines, which included the popular sherry and port.

Sometime in the 1880s, John's sons, John II and Edward, were experimenting with the development of a new sherry. They envisioned a sweeter and richer version that would go well with desserts as opposed to being served as an *aperitif*.

They mixed wine from 50 different soleras, traditional stacked collections of barrels, with the oldest vintages on the bottom, organized to facilitate carefully controlled blending. These included three varieties of sherry – crisp fino, nutty amontillado and fragrant oloroso – along with some Pedro Ximénez sweet wine. They eventually created something they were happy with: a new type of sherry that was sweet, rich and golden brown.

All it needed now was an appropriate name.

Luckily for the brothers, an aristocratic lady visited the Harveys' cellar a few days later. John and Edward gave her a taste of Bristol Milk – a sherry that was popular at the time – and then invited her to try their new blend.

Sipping it cautiously at first, she soon smiled and declared, "Gentleman if that was the milk, then this is the cream."

The enterprising pair adopted the name immediately, and what a good choice it proved to be.

Harveys Bristol Cream is now the best-selling sherry in the world.

SPARKPOINT: *Creating a variation on an existing product, adapted to the needs of a new occasion, can deliver successful innovations.*

71. REAL BEAUTY FOR THE REAL ARMY

The compounds developed for a non-irritating cleaner for the pre-treatment of burns and wounds for the US Army were to become the basis for one of the world's largest personal care brands, whose name and icon are ironically synonymous with peace.

The science behind those treatments led to the creation of the glamorously named Directly Esterified Fatty Isethionate, DEFI for short, which, in turn, led to the development of a synthetic detergent bar that came to be called Dove.

Lever Brothers (now Unilever) launched Dove in 1957 as a new kind of 'beauty' bar. They had determined that increasing numbers of women didn't want to use soap to clean their faces because it dried out their skin.

The brand therefore focused on conveying that Dove was 'much better for your skin' than soap, due to its mildness and the fact that it contained 'one-quarter cleansing cream'. The company ran ads declaring that 'Suddenly soap is old-fashioned!' and 'Dove creams your skin while you wash', focusing on the product's point of difference.

While they constantly compared themselves to soap they never referred to themselves as soap, but rather as a beauty, bath, or bath and toilet bar.

Wanting to further emphasize its difference from traditional soaps, Lever Brothers decided that Dove needed a distinctive shape. They created a novel curved shape that was unlike the rectangular shape of most other soap bars.

The brand and its campaigns evolved over the rest of the 20th century and, while they did dabble with other approaches, most of the company's promotion still revolved around the product's point of difference.

Things, however, changed in April 2004, when the first ads in a completely new campaign appeared. In an era of supermodels and heavily retouched imagery, what made those first posters so different was that they featured six women of different shapes and sizes. They were often curvy and looking more like the women you see every day on the street, not just on the catwalk.

It was the beginning of the 'Real Beauty for Real Women' campaign, one of the most famous brand positionings of the 21st century. Its impact was immediate – there was a 700% spike in Dove sales in the first half of the year after it launched.

Growth has continued and the brand has expanded into many other sectors of the healthcare market. Dove's traditional advertising, digital content and other communications have gathered awards and huge amounts of publicity.

And perhaps coming full circle, in 2010 Unilever launched a range of Dove for men products.

SPARKPOINT: *Giving your brand a bigger vision can provide scope for wider innovation, as it can help you expand into new territories.*

72. THE STORY OF THREE TAILS

In 1988, three Cambridge graduates, Richard Reed, Adam Balon and Jon Wright, were living in London and doing their different day jobs. What they really wanted, however, was to set up their own business and work together on it.

They needed an idea and it came to them from looking at their own lifestyles: like many other 26-year-olds, they were drinking too much beer and eating too much pizza and other takeaway food. They all knew they should try to be healthier but nothing along those lines really appealed to them or fit their lifestyles.

Their idea was all-natural fruit smoothies, which they thought could become 'a great little healthy habit that would make it easy for people to do themselves some good'.

They started experimenting with recipes and after about six months they had a favourite – a combination of orange, banana and pineapple. They initially tested it out on friends and family, who all were very positive.

Still, the three were a bit worried that, "They would say that, wouldn't they?" and decided they needed to test it on other people they didn't know.

The Jazz on the Green festival in Parsons Green was coming up and they thought it would be an ideal occasion to test market their product, as it would attract the type of people their smoothie was aimed at.

They bought £500 worth of fruit, turned it into smoothies, filled little bottles with the beverage and set up a stall.

The original plan was to have a full questionnaire for people to fill out after they'd tried a free sample, but they soon realized that when you're at a festival and it's a lovely sunny day you don't want to fill out a long form. And as they later said, "It felt too corporate."

What they realized was that all they really wanted to know was if people would buy them or not. So, they simplified the research down to one question, which they wrote on a sign: "Do you think we should give up our jobs to make these smoothies?"

They had a 'yes' bin and a 'no' bin, and prior to the event they'd committed to each other that if the yes bin was full they'd quit their jobs the next day. At the end of the day it was clear that the yes bin was full.

The reality of the situation struck home, and suddenly they weren't quite so sure they should give up their safe and lucrative day jobs.

They went back to their house in Barons Court, and there they agreed to see if the gods were on their side.

They would flip a coin to see what they should do – heads meant carry on with the day jobs, tails meant *go for it* and start the new company.

They flipped a coin, not once but three times, and it came up tails every time.

They all went in that Monday morning and resigned. The business they started was Innocent Drinks, one of the most talked about and successful brands of the 'noughties'. Today it sells more than two million smoothies a week and is 90% owned by the Coca-Cola Company.

> **SPARKPOINT:** *Making your idea fit with existing (or at least easy-to-adopt) behaviour will increase its likelihood of success.*

73. THE JOY OF GOOD WINE

Imagine you are a Portuguese vintner at the end of the 19th century and you're looking for new ways to promote your wines and get them to new audiences.

The Great Exhibition of 1874 is being held in the famous Albert Hall and it seems like the ideal event to showcase them, so you choose your best wines and ship the casks over to London.

Now imagine learning some months after the big event that your wines had arrived safely, were stored carefully in the cellars and then … completely overlooked as the big event got under way. Your casks are still sitting in the bowels of the Albert Hall, unseen and untouched.

At this point the Portuguese grower's luck changed a bit when the embarrassed British Government convened a body to do something about the unfortunate oversight. The panel asked a trio of distinguished men to find some way to rectify the situation.

Major-General Henry Scott, one of the architects of the Albert Hall, R Brudenell Carter, a well-known and respected ophthalmic surgeon, and George Scrivenor, a senior official of the Board of Customs, decided to hold a series of lunches to belatedly publicize the wines.

The lunches were a success and many guests went on to purchase the Portuguese wines, helping the grower to achieve his original goal.

However, the success of the event got General Scott wondering if it could be replicated on a bigger and broader scale. He proposed the setting up of 'a co-operative company' to buy good quality wines from around the world and sell them to members.

It was the birth of The International Exhibition Co-operative Wine Society Limited.

The founding members' aim was to buy wines directly from growers to ensure their authenticity and quality, and to offer them to members at fair prices.

The Wine Society, as it is now known, grew slowly and steadily. Its aims were neither size nor profit, but even so by 1965 it was operating out of three separate cellars in London – one under the Palladium, one at Joiner Street under London Bridge and one at Rotherhithe. This prompted the move to consolidate in more suitable premises in Stevenage.

Today, more than 140 years on, The Wine Society continues to be solely owned by its members (one share each) and trades only with them. Life membership is purchased for a one-off fee, and then members are free to buy as much or as little wine as they want.

It continues to be driven not by profit but by its passion for wine, and its purpose is still to celebrate the joy of good wine with its members.

I'll drink to that.

SPARKPOINT: *Can you spot something small but recognize that it is the germ of a bigger idea?*

74. LET THEM EAT CAKE

"Let them eat cake" was supposedly Marie Antoinette's response to being told that the peasants were starving and had no bread.

However, if you are an avid explorer, a rambler or just an occasional walker in the UK's Lake District, when you have 'cake' it is unlikely to be 'an item of soft sweet food made from a mixture of flour, fat, eggs, sugar and other ingredients, baked and sometimes iced or decorated' – the standard definition of cake.

Indeed, a whole shipment of this peculiarly British cake was barred by New York customs in the 1950s and dumped into the Atlantic because it contained neither flour nor eggs.

The cake in question is in fact made from sugar, glucose, water and peppermint oil. While the exact recipe is a secret, it is known that it's made by boiling the ingredients in a copper pan, where the mixture is continuously stirred, and then poured into moulds and allowed to set before being cut into individual bars.

Joseph Wiper, a local Lakeland confectioner, was making a batch of glacier mints (a transparent, boiled mint sweet) but by mistake left the solution standing overnight, whereupon it solidified and became cloudy. Cut into bars, it became the first batch of Wiper's Kendal Mint Cake.

Joseph started production in 1869 and the treat quickly became popular among walkers, climbers and mountaineers as a source of 'concentrated' energy. It has 350 calories per 100 grams.

Sir Ernest Shackleton took the mint cakes on what was to be the first land crossing of the Antarctic. Though unsuccessful, the expedition was recognized as a major feat of endurance and helped reinforce Joseph's product positioning.

The cakes went on to become a popular survival food for expeditions around the world, thanks to their combination of refreshing minty taste and high energy content.

Sir Edmund Hillary, Tenzing Norgay and their team carried Wiper's Kendal Mint Cake with them on the first successful ascent of Mount Everest in 1953, where it was a firm favourite. "We sat on the snow and looked at the country far below us," Sir Edmund said. "We nibbled Kendal Mint Cake."

Another member of the historic Everest expedition wrote: "It was easily the most popular item on our high-altitude ration – our only criticism was that we did not have enough of it." Perhaps that isn't too surprising, given that on the push for the summit of Everest a climber burns an average of 20,000 calories a day (compared with a 'mere' 10,000 a day for the rest of the climb).

George Romney Ltd* confectioners bought Wiper's in 1987 and still produce and sell its Kendal Mint Cake. Today the candy is offered in a number of varieties, including both white and brown sugar, chocolate covered and 'extra strong', for extra flavour at the high altitudes where the taste buds are dulled.

> **SPARKPOINT:** *Combining the same ingredients,*
> *but in new ways, can lead to new ideas.*

---

* The mint cake factory happens to be on Mintsfeet Road North in Kendal, near the River Mint.

75. $400 IPODS WITH $1 EARBUDS

It was a time of change, and legendary record producer Jimmy Iovine – who had worked with John Lennon, U2, Bruce Springsteen, Eminem and others – could sense something in the air.

The industry needed new ideas.

He told his boss, Doug Morris, then the CEO of Universal Music Group, "I can't sell CDs any more. I'm not going to be the guy who sold the last CD, I'm just not that guy." He was intrigued by what Apple and Steve Jobs were doing, seeing it as "making hardware and selling it through software."

Morris gave him license to explore new ventures.

Jimmy picks up the story: "I was walking down the beach one day (in 2006) and I ran into Andre Young, Dr Dre. I was exercising, and I said, 'How're you doing?' And Dre is very soft-spoken, doesn't talk much. He just said to me, 'Yo, my lawyer, he wants me to sell sneakers – what do you think?'"

"I said, 'Dre, nobody in the world cares about how you dress or will care about your sneakers. What you should sell is *speakers*.' At that moment, he said to me, 'We can do that?' And I said, 'F--- yeah.'"

"It all hit me at once: Steve Jobs, the record business, the iPod, Dre, 'cool' ... and I said, 'Let's do this.'"

They soon realized that the future wasn't actually speakers but in headphones. "Apple was selling $400 iPods with $1 earbuds," Iovine recalled. "Dre told me, 'Man, it's one thing that people steal my music. It's another thing to destroy the feeling of what I've worked on.'"

Once prototypes had been developed, Dre used 50 Cent's *In da Club* to test the different options. He chose a bass-heavy version that would make headphones that were truly designed for hip-hop.

"The feeling was that other brands had been developed for more middle-of-the-road rock or even orchestral music," Jimmy said, "and hadn't realized what a lot of people really wanted – music like they would hear in clubs and bars."

Dre tested the headphones with other music genres, listening to everything from Sade to Kraftwerk to make sure that both soul and electronic music sounded right, but he stuck with the bass-rich version. It was something that music critics didn't necessarily like, but which would prove to be popular with buyers.

The new brand needed a name, and that came from Dre and what he thought was the essence of what he did: "I make beats, right, so 'Beats by Dr Dre.'" He would also define the company's guiding principle – to produce a product that reflected his passion for 'perfecting the beat'.

Best Buy in the US became the first big retailer to stock Beats. Brian Dunn, the electronics and home appliance chain's CEO, remembers meeting the founders. "Dre talked about what it was going to mean," he said, "how the industry would get behind it. 'People pay a lot of money for Nikes; they're going to pay money for great headphones that have a great sound, that have some cachet to them.'"

Implicit in this was an important marketing lesson: the competition wasn't really the other headphone brands like Sennheiser or Bose. Rather, Brian came to realize that the question was, "Do I buy the Beats or the Air Jordans? That's the consideration set."

SPARKPOINT: *Different groups of people want the same things, but delivered differently. Addressing this need can be a successful approach.*

SPARKPOINTS

1. The samples they wouldn't give back

SPARKPOINT: *Sometimes you can start out looking for one thing but find another along the way – don't ignore happy accidents.*

2. Drawn to the table by the 'lur' of great butter

SPARKPOINT: *If you have a great idea make sure you do everything to 'own' it, and to protect your ownership of it.*

3. Selling like Wildfire

SPARKPOINT: *Sometimes it's better to go with something that is 80% right than continue to strive for 100% perfect. You might never get there.*

4. Beheading – an unusual source of inspiration

SPARKPOINT: *People can be generous with their ideas, it doesn't cost anything to listen, and sometimes what they say can be of great value.*

5. A story of men and lingerie at Christmas

SPARKPOINT: *Researching your market before you try and enter it can provide valuable lessons, even if you go on to break what appear to be the established rules.*

6. The lesser known sources of inspiration – forgetfulness and embarrassment

SPARKPOINT: *Though a bit of a marketing cliché, a problem isn't always a problem – sometimes it can be an opportunity.*

7. Not an overnight sensation

SPARKPOINT: *Innovation can take inspiration, perspiration and perseverance.*

8. The brand that went down the drain

SPARKPOINT: *If the right supply chain is there, or the current one isn't serving your purpose, you may need to be brave enough to do it yourself.*

9. From books to beauty and the first Avon Lady (who was actually a man)

SPARKPOINT: *Innovation needs you to think not only about who you are going to sell to, but how and by whom that selling should be done.*

10. From wasted to wanted, doing what they said couldn't be done

SPARKPOINT: *One person's waste can be another's inspiration; try to look at things from different perspectives and find new uses.*

11. A second 'eureka' moment – bath time inspiration

SPARKPOINT: *What can you 'borrow' from another market and introduce into your market?*

12. Think sideways – don't let your thinking be constrained

SPARKPOINT: *One innovation can lead to another, so look for ways in which you can further innovate on your original innovation.*

13. In spite of not because of

SPARKPOINT: *Sometimes necessity can be the mother of invention, and putting someone in a difficult situation can actually fire their imagination.*

14. They will never sell

SPARKPOINT: *Innovations need support – they need people who believe in them and will advocate and fight for them, even in the face of resistance.*

15. Love me, love my dog – Zappos on steroids

SPARKPOINT: *Turning your passion into your purpose can be a source of inspiration.*

16. The wasp

SPARKPOINT: *Technical expertise can be transferred into other new sectors. Where could your technical expertise be used to good effect?*

17. The ideal husband – How to win a woman's heart with a bowl of custard

SPARKPOINT: *Solving someone's problem (loved one or not) is a well-used path to innovation.*

18. Go west young man … and moisturize

SPARKPOINT: *Not all ideas will come fully formed, so look at things from different perspectives, and be on the lookout for the germ of a new idea. Can you find a behaviour that is established but where the product isn't obvious?*

19. Beam me up an innovation

SPARKPOINT: *Watching TV, especially if it's a sci-fi series or movie, can be a source of inspiration for future applications of technology.*

20. Toasting the tower

SPARKPOINT: *Can you land a celebrity endorsement of your innovation? It can help enormously.*

21. The curry cycle, a story of 'Indovation'

SPARKPOINT: *Local or regional innovation can be valuable as long as market potential is big enough.*

22. Cauliflowers for tourists – a fair exchange?

SPARKPOINT: *You must not be afraid to adapt your initial idea when a bigger opportunity emerges.*

23. How to create the perfect TV show

SPARKPOINT: *Insightful analysis of big data can be a source of inspiration for innovation.*

24. A picture is worth a billion downloads

SPARKPOINT: *Inspiration can be visual as well as verbal or conceptual. As they say, a picture can be worth a thousand words.*

25. An innovation worth dying for?

SPARKPOINT: *Innovation can call for real commitment.*

26. Doing her homework

SPARKPOINT: *Innovation often requires exploration and experimentation.*

27. A star is born … along with a cow, a dog and a question mark

SPARKPOINT: *Successful innovations should ideally be differentiated from what's already on the market, otherwise why should anyone choose them rather than what already exists?*

28. The sweet smell of success

SPARKPOINT: *Creating a rich sensory experience can add value to your innovation.*

29. After the burn, boom

SPARKPOINT: *Despite the desire for more and more research, sometimes a sample of one is enough.*

30. The queens who stole Barbie's crown

SPARKPOINT: *Though not always easy to achieve, a desire to change the world can be a powerful source of inspiration.*

31. Do one thing and do it properly

SPARKPOINT: *Can you be the first to bring something new to a market, and can you 'steal with pride'?*

32. The prisoner and the broom

SPARKPOINT: *Inspiration can be found anywhere – never stop looking.*

33. Get on your bike and innovate

SPARKPOINT: *Innovation isn't just about new products or services, sometimes it's about doing the same thing but better.*

34. From convent girl to mistress to the sweet smell of success

SPARKPOINT: *If at times you can't do it yourself, don't be afraid to work with relevant experts – but make sure you stay true to what you want.*

35. Launching a brand may not be child's play but it can be a children's book

SPARKPOINT: *Coming up with an idea isn't the only problem, you may need to fight off competition*

36. Why quality is not enough

SPARKPOINT: *If your idea is just about quality it may not be enough – you may need something more to offer your customers.*

37. From beads to boards to becoming a billionaire

SPARKPOINT: *Early prototyping allows you to develop ideas faster.*

38. From biomimicry to metonymy via portmanteau
SPARKPOINT: *Biomimicry is a natural source of inspiration.*

39. Headline news – how to beat the flu
SPARKPOINT: *Keep your ears and your eyes open; you never know what you'll find.*

40. Too sweet?
SPARKPOINT: *A premium version of an existing product can often be an opportunity.*

41. 2M
SPARKPOINT: *Travel is a great source of inspiration.*

42. Le marketing est arrivé: how Beaujolais Nouveau raced to the top
SPARKPOINT: *Though most of the stories in this book are about new products and services, innovation can relate to new forms of communication and activation too.*

43. In the beginning was the word, now there is the app
SPARKPOINT: *Think about how new channels and technology can help you better engage with your audience.*

44. The eyes have it
SPARKPOINT: *People watching is a great source of inspiration – what are they doing and why, and how could that be adapted or improved?*

45. Let them eat tacos

SPARKPOINT: *Inspiration and ideas aren't always about new products; they can help you to run the business better, to make it viable and profitable.*

46. Making an innovation out of a crisis

SPARKPOINT: *How can you take inspiration from a crisis?*

47. A market all sown up

SPARKPOINT: *Working in lots of different jobs can help you take a broader perspective on how to innovate.*

48. Firing your imagination

SPARKPOINT: *Looking for new ways to deliver your brand's long-term vision or purpose can be a source of inspiration.*

49. Turning innovation on its head

SPARKPOINT: *Not all innovations need to be radical – small changes can have big effects. What small changes could you make to help your brand?*

50. A factory in the country – inspired by your principles

SPARKPOINT: *Limiting what you're looking for can sound counterproductive, but it can actually help focus the mind.*

51. From pork chops to ice pops

SPARKPOINT: *Looking for solutions to gaps in your brand's performance can pay dividends.*

52. The key to a new innovation

SPARKPOINT: *Though somewhat obvious, both competitions and the rewards they promise are a great incentive for people to come up with new ideas.*

53. An idea worth every penny

SPARKPOINT: *There are some people who are very good at coming up with new ideas, so one source of 'inspiration' is to hire them or their services.*

54. Every brand needs a little luck

SPARKPOINT: *In a world where time is so important and valuable, a winning innovation often makes something faster.*

55. The young tractor manufacturer and the superstar supercar

SPARKPOINT: *Something that makes you angry can be a great source of inspiration and innovation.*

56. Don't get cold feet

SPARKPOINT: *Combining two things into one is a clever means of innovating.*

57. What you need to do to launch a brand is watch TV

SPARKPOINT: *New ideas may need new production techniques, and you may need to look for inspiration from other industries (or on television!).*

58. He sold seashells

SPARKPOINT: *Inspiration can come from trend watching; the bigger the trend, and the earlier you spot, it the better it is likely to be for you.*

59. Piecing together the jigsaw of an idea

SPARKPOINT: *In Will's own words, "Do something that you actually care about personally."*

60. It's no use crying over spilt chocolate

SPARKPOINT: *When something goes wrong it can be the source of new ideas.*

61. The glue that wouldn't stick

SPARKPOINT: *New technology alone isn't enough – it needs an application that people can truly value.*

62. When one usage isn't enough

SPARKPOINT: *Finding a new use for an existing product, with or without minor modification, can be a source of innovation.*

63. Make it better

SPARKPOINT: *Can you do what someone else does but do it better?*

64. The billion-dollar butt

SPARKPOINT: *If your new idea is going to be sold through retail channels, a good start can be essential.*

65. It takes all sorts

SPARKPOINT: *Variety may not only be the spice of life, but of innovation too. Sometimes more might be more.*

66. Love it or hate it

SPARKPOINT: *Can you turn someone else's by-product into something valuable in its own right?*

67. The godfather of good coffee and his three adopted sons

SPARKPOINT: *Finding and using a mentor can help you learn and avoid problems, but they are also a source of valuable inspiration.*

68. Accidents will happen, but then so can innovations

SPARKPOINT: *Surprisingly, personal misfortune or injury can be a source of inspiration.*

69. A little bit of quality for every street

SPARKPOINT: *Democratizing something that has traditionally been a premium product can deliver big rewards.*

70. Why have milk when you can have 'Cream'?

SPARKPOINT: *Creating a variation on an existing product, adapted to the needs of a new occasion, can deliver successful innovations.*

71. Real beauty for the real army

SPARKPOINT: *Giving your brand a bigger vision can provide scope for wider innovation, as it can help you expand into new territories.*

72. The story of three tails

SPARKPOINT: *Making your idea fit with existing (or at least easy-to-adopt) behaviour will increase its likelihood of success.*

73. The joy of good wine

SPARKPOINT: *Can you spot something small but recognize that it is the germ of a bigger idea?*

74. Let them eat cake

SPARKPOINT: *Combining the same ingredients, but in new ways, can lead to new ideas.*

75. $400 iPods with $1 earbuds

SPARKPOINT: *Different groups of people want the same things, but delivered differently. Addressing this need can be a successful approach.*

THE AUTHOR – GILES LURY

Giles would describe himself as a VW Beetle driving, Lego Watch wearing, Disney loving, Chelsea supporting father of five who also happens to be Director of a leading strategic brand consultancy, The Value Engineers.

He has over 30 years of experience in the business and is known both for his creative spark and his ability to constructively challenge conventional thinking, warranting his other title: Director of Deviancy.

Giles has won two IPA Advertising Effectiveness Awards and a gold medal at the AMSO Research Effectiveness Awards.

He has worked on numerous innovation projects, leading to some major successes and, not surprisingly, the occasional failure. All of this has provided learning experiences for Giles and has been the source of some of his many stories.

He is the author of six previous books, including two volumes of marketing stories – *The Prisoner and the Penguin* and *How Coca-Cola Took Over the World* (both published by LID Publishing).

THE ILLUSTRATOR – GUY CHALKLEY

Guy is often asked if he is an illustrator, a designer, a cartoonist, an innovator or a videographer, and his answer is that he is a combination of all five.

While he has a passion for typography, he's the first to admit that he prefers images to words. And so, when asked to submit something for this biographical blurb, he provided the self-portrait you see here.

Guy has collaborated with Giles Lury on a number of projects at The Value Engineers, the brand consultancy where they both work. He did all 101 illustrations for Giles' last book, *How Coca-Cola Took Over the World*, and being a glutton for punishment (and pies) he volunteered to help on this book too.

ACKNOWLEDGMENTS

As ever, this book would never have happened if it wasn't for help, encouragement and support from lots of people around me.

Thanks to everyone at LID Publishing for their continued support and faith in my writing.

I also appreciate the generosity of colleagues and friends at The Value Engineers for giving me ideas and the space to write. Special mention here should go toan ex-Value Engineer, Paul Walton, who often drops me a link and suggests that there might be a story there.

My heart-felt thanks go to Guy Chalkley, who somehow has produced as many visuals as I have produced stories and still managed to keep a smile on his face. I think his illustrations add enormously to the book.

The kind words of friends who aren't in the business but have liked my previous storybooks have been a spur to keep going, as it's nice to know that I'm not just preaching to the converted.

Last, and of course not least, thanks to my wife and family, who give me the occasional bit of encouragement.

Giles Lury
27/09/18